Hunger for Hope

Hunger for Hope

*Prophetic Communities, Contemplation,
and the Common Good*

Simone Campbell, SSS

ORBIS BOOKS
Maryknoll, New York 10545

Founded in 1970, Orbis Books endeavors to publish works that enlighten the mind, nourish the spirit, and challenge the conscience. The publishing arm of the Maryknoll Fathers and Brothers, Orbis seeks to explore the global dimensions of the Christian faith and mission, to invite dialogue with diverse cultures and religious traditions, and to serve the cause of reconciliation and peace. The books published reflect the views of their authors and do not represent the official position of the Maryknoll Society. To learn more about Orbis Books, please visit our website at www.orbisbooks.com.

Manufactured in the United States of America

Library of Congress Cataloging-in-Publication Data

Names: Campbell, Simone, author.
Title: Hunger for hope : prophetic communities, contemplation, and the
  common good / Simone Campbell, SSS.
Description: Maryknoll, New York : Orbis Books, [2020] | Includes
  bibliographical references.
Identifiers: LCCN 2020002327 (print) | LCCN 2020002328 (ebook) | ISBN
  9781626983786 (trade paperback) | ISBN 9781608338412 (ebook)
Subjects: LCSH: Campbell, Simone. | Sisters of Social Service—Biography. |
  Nuns—United States—Biography. | Women lawyers—United
  States—Biography. | Nuns—Political activity—United States. | Church
  and social problems—United States. | Christianity and justice—Catholic
  Church. | United States—Moral conditions—21st century. | United
  States—Politics and government—21st century.
Classification: LCC BX4705.C2458875 A3 2020 (print) | LCC BX4705.C2458875
  (ebook) | DDC 271/.97 [B]—dc23
LC record available at https://lccn.loc.gov/2020002327
LC ebook record available at https://lccn.loc.gov/2020002328

I pray that this book will be a tribute
to all those whom I have met across the country
who have knowingly or unknowingly nurtured my hope.
Our meetings and story sharing have given me life,
and I am profoundly grateful.

May this small work be a tribute to you
and all that you have given to nourish community.
You, whether you know it or not,
have been a sign of the divine presence for me.

THANK YOU!

Contents

CONTENTS

PART III
EXPRESSIONS OF HOPE

Foreword

Helen Prejean, CSJ

Lucky me, getting to enter ahead of the pack into Simone's grace-filled life to prepare these introductory words. How can I but admire her, she, who woke up so young to the gospel call to forge love of God with love of neighbor, justice with charity, and contemplation with action! If there's perhaps one governing mantra of Simone's life, it is this: get in there close with people on the margins of society and allow your heart to be broken open. It's the breaking open to the raw human need of real people that is for Simone the fire at the heart of her passion for justice. That passion, combined with her contemplative heart, strategic intelligence, and unbreakable bond in community has landed her, as Providence would have it, exactly where she belongs and where in these troubled and confusing times we need her most: Executive Director of NETWORK, our nuns' Catholic Social Justice lobby.

So, praise God, there Simone was at the helm, poised and ready, when pitched congressional arguments broke out over passage of President Obama's Affordable Care Act (ACA) and many, many doubted that it could ever get the votes to pass. For Simone, the mandate for people's need for basic health care came right out of the Gospels, straight from the heart of Jesus, and also right out of the UN Universal Declaration of Human Rights (Thank you Eleanor Roosevelt!). No contest. Get it done. At her urging, my religious community, along with so many other sisters in the country, dove into action: writing letters, signing petitions, and making phone calls to persuade congresspersons to grant passage of the historic act.

I happened to be in Washington, DC, on the day of the ACA's passage and I'm here to tell you that cheers and merrymaking erupted throughout the night, rejoicing that now, at last, poor and middle-class people would be provided one of the most basic of human rights: health care. And there, at the heart of the moral thrust of it all, was Simone.

Nor could I help but notice that the Spirit moving through NETWORK for health care reform is the same driving Spirit that quickens our daily, hourly, year-in-year-out press to end the suffering and torture of state-sanctioned killing. All I can say is: Viva our Sisterhood! And Viva Simone, representing all of us as she attended the signing of the ACA bill by President Obama and in the process got a thankful hug from him. I suspect that every nun in the nation felt that hug. I surely did.

But maybe the best thing of all about Simone, and what I'll always treasure about her and the stalwart crew of NETWORK was the spontaneous, glorious, Spirit-driven inspiration of Nuns on the Bus in 2012, which pulled off a tour to nine states, traveling twenty-seven hundred miles to rouse the people to get out the vote and to prevent the U.S. House of Representatives budget plan to drastically slash social services. The spark that helped inspire the Rolling Community bus tour, as it turns out, was the out-of-the-blue Vatican investigation of American sisters and its special censure of LCWR and NETWORK for "serious doctrinal problems." The investigators claimed that the groups were focusing too much on poverty and economic injustice, while keeping "silent" on abortion and same-sex marriage.

Simone: "We had only nine full-time staff members at the time and we made the whole Vatican nervous? We haven't violated any teaching, we have just been raising questions and interpreting politics." One of the big surprises of the tour was the energetic outpouring along the road of people in support of nuns. One supporter's sign said it all: "Don't mess with our nuns."

As I see it, when the drastic Vatican reprimand of the group was made public, NETWORK wisely kept silent, refusing to defend their orthodoxy with Vatican officials in theological arguments. Instead, they kept their eyes on the prize of the Gospel and got on buses in order to go among the people to help Jesus's justice come through down-to-earth policies and political action. Pure inspiration of the Holy Spirit, I call it.

Then, after April 2015, when the investigation of American nuns was suddenly ended as mysteriously as it had been launched, with no explanation or accountability from Vatican officials, Simone spoke up. While attending a Vatican women's conference in Rome in 2017, even as the cataclysmic Catholic clerical abuse scandal was breaking around the world, Simone spoke truth to power, suggesting that senior clergy at the Vatican seemed more preoccupied with power than with confronting issues that affect the faithful. "These men worry more about the form and the institution than about real people." She said it and she was done, not elaborating on the subject, not stretching out the debate because the investigation was ended and nuns had "won." No such waste of energy on internal Church arguments for Simone. The real needs of suffering people call to us for action.

Hunger for Hope is rich with Simone's spiritual encounters with Christ. Her soul is wide—she practices Zen meditation—and the real-life engagements to which those encounters lead her couldn't be shared with us at a better time.

Feeling hopeless and powerless and "fake-newsed-out"? Wondering how to make Catholic faith come to life in this perplexing and divided world?

Welcome into Simone's mind and heart, and, best of all, her feet-on-the-ground manual for making the Gospel come alive in the real, real world.

Acknowledgements

This work would not exist without the invitation of Paul McMahon and Robert Ellsberg of Orbis Books and the opportunity to give a summer workshop at St. Mary's in South Bend, Indiana. It is built on the work of Old Testament scripture scholar, Walter Brueggemann. I am not certain that he will recognize his influence, but his scholarship is at the heart of my work in community.

My religious community, the Sisters of Social Service, have, through all these years, made me the person I've become. Without our "Life in the Spirit," I am adrift. I am so grateful for the nourishment and insight (and struggle) that my sisters provide. It is indeed a gift.

It is through NETWORK, Lobby for Catholic Social Justice, that I have been able to live out my commitment to live Catholic social teaching. NETWORK is my ministry of lobbying on Capitol Hill and speaking around the country. The staff and members of NETWORK have been an invaluable support in writing this book. They have provided feedback and suggestions as well as moral support. I am especially grateful to Colleen Ross, who leads our communications team, and Lee Morrow, our press secretary. They helped give this book life.

Finally, to all of the people across the country who have told me their stories, shared their joys and griefs, and been community in challenging times: THANK YOU! Thousands of people have been a part of our Nuns on the Bus campaigns. Without you, our work would not be possible. You give NETWORK life. You give this book life! Together, we can be the hope for which we hunger.

Introduction

I never set out to be anything but faithful. It has been a surprising journey, but not all that unique. I have come to see that, although my experience may seem mundane, it is critical that I give it voice, and I encourage you to do the same with your experience. In the face of the political and social crises of our time, I believe that, at the heart of it all, we as a nation—and maybe even as a church—face a spiritual crisis. Unless we embrace the challenge of faithfulness in these chaotic times, I believe that we are lost. But I am getting ahead of myself. Let me start at the beginning.

The Foundation

I grew up in southern California as the eldest of four. I went to Catholic school and learned early on that the Gospel was not an old book, but rather a living reality. I have always known that faith has consequences. As a young person, I listened to Dr. Martin Luther King Jr. on television. I saw young people in Birmingham stand up for civil rights. Both my sister Katy and I knew that civil rights were important.

We also knew that these rights were integrally connected to faith.

When my sister was a sophomore and I was a senior in high school, Katy was diagnosed with Hodgkin disease and given three to five years to live. Needless to say, this shocking event changed everything in our family. Katy fully lived those five years. For myself, I have come to know that, in her dying, I picked up some of her spirit and urgency. In some ways, I have lived with two intensities.

This double intensity led me to join my religious community, the Sisters of Social Service. We were founded in Budapest, Hungary, in 1923 and in Los Angeles in 1926. We are dedicated to the Holy Spirit and, therefore, open to a spirituality that trusts the movement of the Spirit more than the strictures of the rules.

The focus of our work as a community is to embody the social teaching of the church through meeting the unmet social needs of our time. We have always been about responding to such needs without creating big institutions. We are creative and pioneering in responding to the pressing needs around us.

It is from this tradition that I set out to write this book. My more extensive memoir, published in 2014, *A Nun on the Bus: How All of Us Can Create Hope, Change, and Community*, chronicles my journey in greater detail. This book shares the spiritual lessons that I have learned over more than fifty years of religious life and contemplative practice. It is not an academic treatise or a compendium of prayer techniques. Rather, it is the result of my experience amid a politically chaotic time. My fondest hope is that this effort might give others the courage to talk about their own experience.

Briefly, you should know that as a Sister of Social Service I did social work for a few years. In the process, I discovered that I was not the best social worker. I did not have the patience needed to be truly effective. However, my work in community organizing and social policy led me to realize that I had an interest in practicing law.

After taking final vows, I enrolled at the University of California Davis School of Law. Once I had graduated and passed the California bar, I opened the Community Law Center to serve working poor families in Oakland, California. Our clients were those who did not qualify for free legal service but could not afford private counsel. We charged everyone on a sliding scale based on income and number of dependents.

I loved this work. We handled most of the high-conflict, low-income family law cases in the county. Because of crowded court calendars, I learned how to quickly summarize a case and make my most compelling argument to a judge. I cared for my clients and worked with them to improve their family circumstances, especially those having to do with their children. I gained a deeper understanding of family dynamics. Repeatedly, I "listened deeply" to my clients' needs in order to be effective in their lives.

COMMUNITY LEADERSHIP

After eighteen years of practicing law, I realized that the Law Center was like my child. During this time, it had grown from just me to an organization employing six attorneys and six paralegals, as well as support staff. For it to flourish, it seemed to me that I should leave so that my partners, who had more skills in administration, could take the Law Center to the next level. I, with my talent for innovation and creativity, had some ideas of what else I could do to respond to social needs However, my community elected me to be general director of our small international community for a five-year nonrenewable term.

My sisters taught me much during those years of leadership. One of the most painful lessons early in my term was that I was seen as too "corporate" and not a spiritual leader. This shocked and hurt me. But in good prayer practice, I took this pain to meditation, knowing that if it hurt me it was because there was some truth in the criticism.

What I came to learn was that I was a spiritual leader, but my sisters did not know this because I never talked about my spiritual journey or insights. My sisters have since taught me to speak of the spiritual journey and the challenges that we face. It is this learning that has led directly to my writing of this book.

I can talk policy and politics for hours on end. I can debate the benefits of different health care proposals or what housing policy will be good for low-income families. But my insight in this moment is that, if I do not speak of the spiritual practices and insights that are essential for today, then I am betraying the challenge of the Spirit to live in relationship with the people who are most in need in our time.

Politics

Through my ministry I have been given a unique exposure to the needs of the people of our nation, and to the political realities involved in responding to those needs. In 2004, I was recruited to be the executive director of NETWORK Lobby for Catholic Social Justice. NETWORK began in 1972 as an organization to weave together the federal advocacy work of Catholic Sisters in the United States. I was the fourth executive director in almost thirty years. Our mission is to lobby for just legislation on Capitol Hill and in the administration. From our beginning, we have worked on a variety of economic, justice, and peace-building issues.

In 2010, NETWORK received notoriety when, in support of the Affordable Care Act (ACA), we released a letter signed by fifty-nine Catholic Sisters who held leadership positions in their religious congregations. Because many of the signers' congregations sponsored health systems, their support for the ACA was based on their extensive knowledge of the ins and outs of health policy. The United States Conference of Catholic Bishops (USCCB) had come out opposing the bill two days before we released our letter. In the end, the Affordable Care Act was passed and benefited almost twenty-five million people in our country. This "nuns vs. bishops" view of the media garnered NETWORK a fair amount of publicity at the time. After all the media ruckus had died down, I thought we had "moved on."

In April of 2012, we celebrated the fortieth anniversary of NETWORK. At the celebration the big question was, "How are we going to let people know that we have been lobbying on Capitol Hill for forty years?" We had a lot of little ideas. However, four days after our celebration, we received from Rome an answer to our prayer. The Vatican issued a censure of the Leadership Conference of Women Religious (LCWR) and identified our little organization,

NETWORK, as a bad influence on Catholic sisters. We responded with prayer, conversation, and action.

The result of the censure was an explosion of interest in Catholic sisters. NETWORK's Nuns on the Bus campaign was a direct result of this notoriety. It is true that it was painful to be so misunderstood by the Vatican. However, there were other benefits. Because there were places around the country where we could not speak on church diocesan property, we went to our interfaith partners. For NETWORK, this resulted in an expansion in terms not only of numbers of members but also of their diversity. We learned that being faithful to mission led to surprising growth and opportunities. It felt like a Pentecost event, one in which we had been huddled together in fear and then tossed out onto the rooftops and roads to speak our truth about the needs of struggling families throughout the country and how Republican policies (principally Congressman Ryan's budget) were going to make their lives worse.

This adventure of Nuns on the Bus has included six bus trips over seven years. We have had various themes for each our trips, including the federal budget, immigration reform, tax policy, voter turnout, and bridging the divides in political conversation. Each trip has deepened our awareness of the struggles of our time and the joy that is possible in being together in community. These trips have made us aware of the worry and loneliness that characterize our polarized nation.

On the first trip, during a stop in Hershey, Pennsylvania, a woman in her mid-thirties wanted to know whether, if she joined NETWORK, we could give her the names of some people in her area with whom she could talk about things she cared about. It made me want to weep. How have we become so divided and so far from each other?

The bus has woven my spirituality into the reality of encounter. Taking time to listen to the stories of people in different parts of the nation fuels our commitment to work for justice for everyone—the 100 percent. Each stop on our routes has been seared into my memory. As the sisters create community among themselves and the staff, that community begins to include everyone we meet along the way. It is a community that nurtures all of our lives and moves us in new directions, both in politics and in how we care for one another.

THE CURRENT CRISIS

The current political chaos is not just a political crisis; it is also a spiritual crisis. The political crisis is fueled by a president who is lost in his own ego and sees no suffering outside his own. However, the deeper issue is that people voted for him as president. It is true that he lost the popular vote, but he got sufficient votes to be elected. This means that we need to look at the underlying reality, what it was that made this chaotic, reactionary, and hostile personality attractive to voters in our nation. Politics alone cannot answer this question. In my view, the answer lies in a deeper place and has to do with a spiritual crisis that we are facing as a nation—a crisis spawned by the corrosive lie that our foundation, both as people and as a nation, is individualism. It is this lie that is sucking the life out of the heart of our nation.

Spirituality is at the core of our daily lives and struggles. It is the values we live by and the care that we take of each other. For me, this spirituality is rooted in the Catholic tradition, but I have come to learn that there are many ways to be open to the divine presence in our midst. In my experience, it is this divine presence that knits us together. You do not have to be Christian or Catholic for this journey. You just have to be open to a story that is bigger than your own.

If we are faithful, we can connect with each other in surprising ways. We can even turn back from the destructive path that we are on and find a way to weave our society back together. We need to stay faithful to the spiritual journey that challenges us to be aware of the needs of others and to care for our earth. In the face of the pain and crises of this political time, I cannot be silent, nor can any of us. We must share with each other. Our sharing needs to be rooted in faith and in mutual connection. Only then will we be strong enough to engage together the challenges of our time.

The current chaos is sometimes overwhelming. I yearn to avert my eyes from the often-grim reality. I don't want to hear the dehumanizing slogans chanted by our leaders. I am horrified by the policies that tear children from their parents and demonize immigrants. I am shocked that elected leaders lie with impunity. The communal sins of racism, anti-Semitism, and Islamophobia are eroding whatever moral fabric we have left as a nation. But I cannot turn away.

I ask: What is happening to our nation? How are we to deal with these impossible circumstances? It strikes me that we as a nation have a life-threatening illness. We are soul-sick in our individualism and heart-sick in our emotional/

spiritual distance from each other. I encounter anguish at every turn. So, in the face of our national anguish, join me as I share what I have learned on the journey.

Exploring a Toxic Environment

The crassness of our current political leaders is undermining our democracy. It touches an anger that is crippling so many of our people, especially in small towns and rural communities. Anger and fear are making our nation more violent, yet political leaders are addressing neither the source of the anger nor the ease with which angry people can get access to guns.

Just as our civic leaders are failing us, many people view our religious institutions as untrustworthy. The clergy abuse scandal has undermined the Catholic Church. The incapacity of our church leaders to offer spiritual leadership is crippling the church's capacity to minister to this pain-ridden world. The hierarchy's fixation on rules and conservative politics has torn the heart out of any response in this time of spiritual crisis.

Our leaders, both secular and religious, are failing us to the extent that I find myself often paralyzed in the face of the anger and hate.

In 2015, I was invited to give a talk at a small Christian college in southern Indiana. The committee sponsoring the lecture gathered in a sun-drenched living room for informal conversation before the lecture. One of the women on the planning team brought a flyer that had been put in her rural mailbox. It was an advertisement for joining the Ku Klux Klan. I could barely touch the paper. It had a shocking caricature of President Obama and stated clearly that he should not be president...and should be shot! How do we live in a world with such hate?

I recall a man I met in Indianapolis in 2016. A rugged machinist in his fifties, he told me with great exuberance that he was for Donald Trump for president. I asked him why. His reply was telling: "I saw him on television, and he is tough!" The man went on to describe the TV show *The Apprentice* and how Mr. Trump had said to people "You're fired!"

I asked him why he felt that "toughness" was so important.

He proceeded to tell me some of his story. While he was growing up, his parents had told him that if he "worked hard and played by the rules" he would get ahead. But this had not been the case. He had worked hard but was still struggling. His two kids were having an even harder time. They had gone to college but had to move back home because they could not find good paying jobs. They could not pay rent AND pay off their student debt. They were struggling, so the whole family was working to help them.

As he spoke, he kept returning to his parents' "promise."

After a nudge from the Holy Spirit, I asked him if perhaps he felt ashamed that he had not measured up to his parents' expectations. Suddenly, he got tears in his eyes. It startled both of us!

What I realized in the exchange was that his anger and his need for "toughness" were connected to his feeling that he was a failure. He had not fulfilled his parents' expectations. He felt that he had failed his parents and his kids. He had accepted the fallacy that we are all simply individuals struggling on our own. This misconception, this view that individualism is the cornerstone of our nation, is under-mining our society by making our people blind to the sys-temic reality that is shifting money to the top of the economic ladder and hurting everyone else.

THE LIE OF INDIVIDUALISM

President Reagan, through clever commercials, shifted our founding narrative from the story of a communitarian genesis to one based on rugged individualism. He stated that we each must take care of ourselves, and offered us the image of the lone white man riding off on his horse to "settle" the West. This was the myth—or dare I say lie—that he sold to the American people.

We know that no single individual created our nation or our communities. No individual raised a barn or com-pleted a quilt. Jamestown was a community of people struggling together, and the Pilgrims came by the shipload to create a colony. The indigenous people living on this land when the Europeans arrived had strong communal bonds, and in the beginning were able to help the Euro-pean settlers.

But the lie of individualism was a better fit for Presi-dent Reagan's political rhetoric. He successfully embel-lished it by stigmatizing struggling families that were not earning enough to get by. Building on the endemic racism in our nation, President Reagan then proceeded to create another myth, that of the "welfare queen." The myths had all been invented to support what was in essence a lie.

Forty years later, we are experiencing the consequences of this lie. We have an eroded sense of community. We continue to perpetuate a racism that leaves out and alienates large groups of our people.

What do we do when our leaders have lost their moral voice? When our leaders are silent or endorse hateful attitudes? What do we do when civic leaders undermine the very institutions that have allowed us to prosper as a nation for almost 250 years? What do we do when our religious leaders are not voicing moral truths? To whom can we look amid these civic and moral crises?

Ordinary action and power politics are not the answer. Something more is required. We have reached a point at which it is clear that we ourselves must take responsibility. We are the leaders we have been waiting for!

To engage in the struggle that faces us, we need a contemplative approach. I have come to see that only from deep listening to the Holy Spirit—a still, small voice or a whispering breeze—will we be able to find our way through the chaos and work effectively for change. In this book I attempt to share how I came to this insight through my work for justice and my experience of more than fifty years in religious life.

The book is divided into three parts. The first, "The Contemplative," outlines both the "how" of a contemplative practice as well as its benefits. The next section, "The Community," explores what is necessary to create a community that nurtures a prophetic imagination. This type of imagination is essential if we are going to find a way out of the mire of our political time. In the final section, "Expressions of Hope," I apply some of the insights of the first two sections to two critical issues of our time. It is in the application of faith lived in community to current struggles that we come to experience true hope.

My own hope is that, by lifting up the nexus of the contemplative life and the work of justice, we will find a new enthusiasm and a renewed faith and confidence that God is alive in our time.

Part I

The Contemplative

1

The Practice

It is frightening to write about my perspective of the contemplative life. It is the most intimate part of my being, and expressing it so directly makes me feel very vulnerable. I am rarely able to look at the Divine directly, and so I usually tend to view the Divine out of the corner of my eye, with a sideways glance or just a niggling intuition. To say anything more feels presumptuous. Nevertheless, my contemplative practice has led me to this moment of risk taking. What are my feelings of personal vulnerability in the face of the needs of our time?

The great twentieth-century theologian Karl Rahner once stated: "In the future Christians will be contemplatives or they will not be at all." This truth drives me with a fierce urgency to share my story and urge you to share yours.

I am a practitioner of the contemplative way, not a theoretician. While my contemplative practice may often seem muddled and distracted, it is important. Over the past thirty-five years or more, it has become the foundation of who I am and impacts every aspect of my existence. Rather than being about hiding out in the chapel for hours on end, my contemplative practice has led me to an activism that is expansively grounded in compassion and care for others.

When I first began to meditate in the Zen style, I worried that I would become detached and "ethereal." In fact, I have experienced the opposite; the practice has led me deeper into political action and encounter. It has become the vibrant core of my being. However, I had never talked about the practice. I just did it.

It was not until the first decade of this century, when I heard Fr. Michael Crosby, OFM Cap, speak about being a contemplative, that I had the courage even to name my practice. Gradually, as I encountered our society's need for a spiritual grounding, I became more public in mentioning it in my talks and even in daily conversation. Now, on some mornings when an idea about work has wandered into my awareness during meditation, I am likely to say to a staff member, "I had an idea during my distracted meditation this morning."

The urgency of our current times gives me the boldness to write about my contemplative journey. I offer this simple truth: the exuberant Divine holds us at every moment. But let me first explain how I got to the revelation of this truth.

My Journey

By nature, I am reflective and get insights in a highly intuitive fashion. After opening a legal practice to serve the working poor families of Oakland, California, in 1977, I started dabbling in centering prayer. At first, I listened to tape recordings by Fr. Basil Pennington and Fr. Thomas Keating. I hungered to live a grounded spirituality that could sustain me in the risk-taking creation of the law center and practicing law.

In 1983, my community sponsored a long weekend retreat with Fr. Willigis Jaeger, OSB. Fr. Willigis was both a Benedictine priest and a Zen *roshi* (teacher). During those five days, I found the Zen prayer practice that spoke to my being. The experience was like that of diving off a high diving board into a refreshing pool. This pool became my contemplative practice.

Following this initial experience, most mornings I would take time to meditate. Sometimes I would think that I did not have time for a "full" twenty minutes, so I would only do ten. But, despite this bargaining, I was moderately faithful to the practice, and often made annual Zen retreats in this "bilingual" (Christian content/Buddhist style) fashion. But, I have never talked about it directly ... until now.

There are many "how to" meditation books and online resources. But I feel compelled to write of my practice because it is the only way I know to find any sort of stability in the current political chaos. Tossed by daily disturbing headlines and tweets, it is only through a contemplative practice that I have any sort of balance or equilibrium.

Let me briefly describe my own practice of meditation. The most important thing, though, is to try it yourself and allow yourself to be led by the whispers of the Spirit. Trust what comes to you in this time of silence—I have found that it is usually Spirit-given. You will be accompanied at every breath—whether you are aware of it or not.

The Process of Meditation

The first step in contemplative practice is to make space for silence. Put away the cell phone and all the buzzers and notifications that often fill our lives. Turn off the news, the podcast, and the computers that occupy our attention. Contemplative practice is often best first thing in the morning. For me, it is the easiest time to let go of all the other thoughts that crowd my day. Set aside an area as your habitual place to meditate. I have a corner of my room that has a little "altar"—actually, a trunk covered with a cloth and various artifacts. I use a prayer cushion (*zafu*), partially because I was introduced to a contemplative practice through Zen, and I face a blank wall to minimize external distractions.

I set a timer for twenty-five minutes, but you can choose whatever amount of time makes sense for you. Start with ten or fifteen minutes. The most important thing is to start!

In meditation, making space for physical silence is only one part of the experience. It is also important to quiet the body. In an erect posture, I can sit in stillness for long periods. If you are tempted to fidget, take a deep breath and do not give in to the urge. Sometimes (or often) I get concerned that my timer has stopped, and I want to check it. When I feel this urge, I take a deep breath and restate my desire to be open to the Divine in all things…even the distractions!

Sit straight so that you can breathe deeply. A key to doing this is sitting so that your knees are a bit lower than your hips. Try to imagine a string pulling at the crown of your head that gets your head, shoulders, and lower back in line. Your lower back should tilt in a little to give you the balance of an "S" curve. This is the balance you need for stillness. Take a deep breath. And, as you breathe out, set your desire on being silent and open to the Divine. Sometimes, I just say that I am hungry for an awareness of the sacred.

After focusing on becoming present, I try to be open and listen through my body to the Divine. Sometimes, it is good to have a word or mantra to use as I breathe. It gives my mind a focus while I try to be open. This mantra can be an expression of desire or spiritual openness. Trust what comes to mind and breathe with the word(s).

Over time, my word has shifted and changed as my life and insights have changed. For a while, my mantra was "Lead kindly light" from a poem by Saint John Henry Cardinal Newman. I would breathe in on the word "lead" and breathe out slowly on the words "kindly light." More recently, it is a line from Gerard Manley Hopkins's poem, "God's Grandeur": "Flame out like shining from shook foil." Some people tell me that they use the word "Jesus" or a line from scripture, such as, "Lord, that I may see." Trust whatever word fits you...or, as some say, the word that finds you. There are times when my word is quite simple: "Help!"

Do not expect fireworks in this form of meditation. Most days are very quiet. Every now and then there might be some insight or awareness that is important and sets a direction. However, know that the consistent practice brings a profound openness to others and a willingness to risk for the common good.

STUMBLING BLOCKS

I have also learned that my resistance to doing this form of meditation rises regularly. I say to myself, "I should be more quiet," or "I shouldn't look at the timer," or "I should spend more time meditating!" Gerald May in *Will and Spirit* offers important advice. When we are resisting this form of prayer, it is because our egos know that they will be changed by it, and they resist. Gerald May recommends that, rather than beating ourselves up with criticism, we say to our beleaguered selves, "It's okay, ego. I know you are resisting because you don't want to change." After acknowledging this, ask the divine Spirit for help. In my experience, such acknowledgment reduces my resistance and opens me anew to the quiet.

Acknowledging resistance also helps me to accept that I am not in control. My "grasshopper mind" should be enough for me to figure that out, but I often think that I am able to take care of whatever arises in the silence. Repeatedly, I have found that this is not true. It is my illusion of control, an illusion that I need to relinquish.

In the gospel story of the transfiguration, Peter, James, and John go up the mountain with Jesus. A cloud overshadows them. In the cloud, Moses and Elijah appear talking to Jesus. A voice from the cloud says, "This is my Son, the Beloved; listen to him!" (Mark 9:2–8). Peter is elated and suggests that they erect three tents, one for each of the great teachers. Peter wants to hold on to this moment and literally pitch a tent there. Then the scripture says that Peter and the other two apostles "were terrified" (9:7). Ah, the human response! When approaching the sacred, we want to stay close and, at the same time, we cower in fear. What ambivalence— but both responses shut down the contemplative experience.

On our contemplative journey, the gospel account of the transfiguration teaches that the two attitudes that block contemplative experience are holding on (efforts at control) and fear. I used to think that I held on only when I was afraid, but I have found that it is also tempting to hold on to good experiences. If I have my hands wrapped around one experience, I do not have open hands to receive what is coming toward me. If I am afraid, then I am focused on myself, and I lose a sense of the other.

I learned this in 2012, when my life became more public during the notoriety generated by the Vatican censure. I had myriad of experiences that I savored. I had the good fortune to appear on the television show *The Colbert Report*. I was a speaker at the 2012 Democratic Convention. I got to go to Rome, where I received a Democracy Award from the International Parliamentarians for Global Action. These are but a few of the dazzling adventures I had! It was a life rich in gifts.

My contemplative practice led me to realize that I was feeling tempted to hold on to all of these good things. I wanted to stop and savor the delight, the attention. It was difficult to appropriately enjoy and marvel at these myriad experiences without letting my ego get puffed up! I was aware of wanting to bring these delights up in conversation repeatedly. This made the experiences about me and made me "special."

Being "special" undercuts the contemplative life because it pulls us away from the contemplative truth that we are one. In my case, it changed my awareness from being about the gift to being about me. Holding on to "special" experiences was pulling me away from the core of my life. I came to realize that if I was grasping some special memory, if I was holding on to good things, then I was not open to receiving new experiences.

WILLINGNESS

Over the years I have learned that the only thing that I bring to this journey is a willing heart. In reality, willingness is central. Willingness will lead us to the truth of the hunger of our time. Willingness gets us into unexpected situations, and willingness is at the heart of the journey into mystery.

In practicing willingness, I have wondered at the "old ways" that are not working. I have noticed that the old "obey the laws" approach of my childhood has become hollow and ineffective. Contemplative practice has led me to see that the twenty-first century is much more ambiguous and complex. My experience of life is not simple. Day after day, I hear new stories that open me to the deeper complexity of our time.

It was refreshing to read Sr. Ilia Delio's book, *Making All Things New*, in which she states that society and the church are moving away from the static concepts of the "laws of nature" and the "laws of God." In the 1600s, both were seen as fixed and immutable. With Einstein, we have come to see that many of the things that we considered fixed and immutable—such as space and time—are not in fact so. Sr. Ilia notes that we are in the process of absorbing the findings of quantum physics into our culture and faith. Thanks to recent scientific discoveries, we have come to realize that matter and energy are different forms of the same reality. Teilhard de Chardin had early glimpses of this. He saw all of creation converging in Christ. It was a contemplative insight at the heart of our longing for a way to express the reality proclaimed by St. Paul: "All creation groans in one great act of giving birth" (Rom 8:22).

This groaning has left many religious leaders out of touch. While it is not just the Catholic Church that is involved in the struggle, it is this church's experience that I know best. As in other traditions, many in the hierarchy of the Catholic Church were trained to believe that spiritual leadership is enforcing the "laws of God." But this approach does not work in the twenty-first century.

Pope Francis is attempting to change some of the legalistic thinking, as evidenced in his statement, "Who am I to judge?" Such a shift is not easy. Those who were successful in enforcing the "rule of law" are having an extremely difficult time turning to the deeper reality of the vibrant contemplative truth that the Divine is alive in our midst.

If the leadership of the church focuses only on the rules, then it risks alienating many, because it ignores the urgent reality and needs of our time. In my travels across the country I have met people who feel driven from the institutional church by the judgment of the hierarchy and a lack of real spiritual guidance. Their anguish saddens me deeply. What the Book of Proverbs says is true: "Where there is no vision, the people perish" (29:18 KJV). Many, if not most, of our church leaders do not have the insight or vision needed for twenty-first-century leadership. In these challenging times, it is up to us.

So I invite you to accompany me as we seek a contemplative way forward through the moral and civic quagmire in which we find ourselves. Let us not be afraid. Let us open ourselves to the mystery that abounds in our midst. Through contemplative practice we will come to know that the Spirit is alive, that we are not alone. By walking willingly into the world, we can be open in new ways to the anguish of our times. This is the contemplative life. Let us live in that Spirit in our chaotic world that is so hungry for hope.

QUESTIONS FOR REFLECTION

What is my contemplative practice?

Where do I find silence and space in my life to "listen with the ear of my heart"?

What is my resistance to contemplative practice?

How am I "groaning" in one great act of giving birth?

2

Deep Listening

A couple of years ago, an experience allowed me to have a better understanding of the heart of my spiritual practice. I was being interviewed by Fr. James Martin, SJ, someone I deeply admire for his work as a faith leader who speaks from the heart of his own lived experience. I was eager to have a conversation with him about the intersection of faith and the public square. He began with what he considered an easy question. He asked me to share my "favorite story of Jesus." Usually I am very nimble in interviews, but this time I could not think of a single scripture story! We were both surprised.

Laughing, I finally responded that my community was dedicated to the Holy Spirit, so could he ask me about the Holy Spirit. This led to an interesting discovery for us both: the gifts of our religious communities deeply impact our views of the world. His Jesuit community is dedicated to Jesus and therefore focused on the gospel story; my community focuses on Pentecost and the post-Pentecost vibrancy of the Holy Spirit alive in our world.

It is the Pentecost story from the Acts of the Apostles that got the Church (and my religious community) started. The story relates how the followers of Jesus were huddled together in the upper room. They were frightened because Jesus, their leader, had been killed, and they were worried about what would happen to them. They did not know what to do. They had seen Jesus after his death . . . and then he was gone. So they were huddled together, afraid.

The story goes that as they were gathered in the upper room there was suddenly the sound as of a mighty wind, and tongues of fire appeared above each person's head. All at once their fear vanished. They felt compelled to leave the room and announce Jesus's message of love and community. Peter, the formerly tongue-tied leader, was transformed into an eloquent preacher in his proclamation of the message. It is said that he was "filled with the Holy Spirit" (Acts 2:4). This Pentecost mandate to go out beyond our fears is at the heart of my faith experience and my contemplative practice. It is also at the heart of my religious community.

My discussion with Fr. Jim got me to reflect on my meditation practice. I have realized that I do not often focus on scripture stories. Rather, my experience has become a "deep listening" to the signs of the times and the anguish of the moment. This deep listening is in quiet and stillness. I trust what starts to emerge, even if it is a distraction.

LISTENING IN THE SILENCE

Deep listening is being attentive to the "still, small voice" that whispers insights or nudges for action. It helped me care for my clients at the law center and with opposing attorneys. It got me to work systemically in family law to improve the court systems in California. It sustained me in challenging times in the practice of law.

This is the same still, small voice that whispered when the Vatican censured the Leadership Conference of Women Religious and accused our small organization, NETWORK, of being a bad influence on Catholic sisters in the United States. At the time I talked with many of our colleagues who work in faith-based organizations. We held a gathering of prayer, sadness, and worry about the censure for our interfaith partners and secular colleagues. We tried to be a community connected in a challenging time.

However, all of my friends in the faith community were feeling frustrated, angry, and despondent. We were caught and could not break loose from this circle of depression.

While I was meditating, the story of Jesus and the Samaritan woman at the well came to mind. In good meditation practice, I tried to let it go. It kept coming back. After my quiet time, the story continued to nag me, so I finally looked up John 4:4–42, where the story is told.

In the story, Jesus is traveling back to Galilee from Judea and passes through the foreign territory of Samaria. As a Jew, he is not supposed to talk to Samaritans. And, being a man, he is not supposed to talk to women—especially a woman alone. Not only does he break all the rules in speaking with this Samaritan woman, he also asks for her help.

In pondering this scripture passage, I came to understand its message: go out beyond the religious community. Thus, I reached out to our secular colleagues for assistance in this difficult time. I invited them to a meeting in our office to help us discern a way forward. It was their insight at an hour-and-a-half meeting that created Nuns on the Bus. They said that we had to go on the road, lift up the work of

Catholic sisters, and continue pushing back against the Ryan budget as we had been doing. For me, it was a Pentecost moment! I was thrust beyond my fear of the Vatican censure and out into our nation to proclaim a message of love and inclusion. This very mixed group of secular colleagues was of one mind and one heart. I knew immediately that we had to act.

I told the group that we could not go public with our plan until we had raised the money to cover the costs. I was nervous, because during the 2008 recession and following it, money had been very tight for NETWORK. We were barely scraping by. But this was a Spirited moment; we had the money pledged in ten days!

I wondered how we would get publicity. The day after the planning meeting, one of my colleagues who had been at the meeting in DC happened to meet with the religion reporter for the *New York Times*. My colleague told her about our plans and later urged me to follow up with her. I called and the reporter asked me for an "exclusive." In my view, these were more gifts of the Spirit in challenging times. And a couple of weeks later, the *New York Times* broke the news that we were going on the road. It was a front-page story with a photo!

All of this resulted from listening to and trusting the still, small voice and acting on what I had heard.

At times, deep listening can be surprising. Sometimes I feel like Elijah in the First Book of Kings (19:11–13). Initially, he looks for the Lord in the wind, and then in the earthquake, and then in the fire. He is surprised that God is in none of these. Rather, he finds the Divine finally in a "sound of sheer silence." It is this murmuring sound that inspires him to get on the correct path and be ready to act.

ACTIVISM AND LISTENING

It is not just during meditation that the practice of listening is beneficial. It is also beneficial when I am in conversations or on lobby visits. Deep listening means listening to others without judgment. It takes effort to "get inside someone else's skin" or "walk in another's shoes." Listening without judgment allows new ideas to emerge in unexpected moments.

For example, by 2018 our efforts at NETWORK had made it apparent that health care, economic opportunity, housing, and a variety of other concerns were in crisis in our nation. When we considered these issues more closely and looked at a map depicting where the crises were most intense, we discovered that they were most often found in rural communities. Looking at the needs without judgment led to the emergence of a new idea in our planning. We realized that most of us at NETWORK are "city folk"—or at least suburban folk!—and that although we had preconceived notions regarding rural reality, we really did not know it first-hand. As we engaged in prayerful listening, it became clear that we needed to hear from people actually living in rural communities. Consequently, we dedicated the following year to creating a series of listening sessions in rural communities around the nation to learn the needs of people in rural America. By listening, we have learned a tremendous amount and our imaginations have been stirred.

One of the listening sessions I attended was held in a Methodist church founded in 1845 in Poetry, Texas! A group of eight people had gathered for a roundtable to discuss with me their experience in their rural community. One of them arrived a little late, and he explained that he had been helping his neighbor get his mower out of a ditch. Another had brought with her a casserole that she planned on sharing with a sick neighbor after our session. A third talked about having to call a neighbor to let her know that "a cow was down." These were among the comments made by the various participants. It was obvious that they simply understood the comments as part of a neighborly conversation, an ordinary conversation about their lives.

After a while, we spoke about the fact that there are no grocery stores in the area. There are only a couple of Dollar General stores that sell canned goods. The situation is made worse by the fact that many people commute an hour and a half or more into Dallas for work. After work they stop at grocery stores in the city before returning home. This means not only that their grocery dollars remain in the city but also that local stores cannot stay in business because there is not enough local business volume.

I pointed out that Supplemental Nutrition Assistance Program (SNAP) benefits can have a strong positive impact on rural communities because they channel much-needed new dollars into small economies. I thought this was a great way of showing how key federal programs for low-income families can benefit the whole community.

On hearing this, one of the participants got really upset. "People need to take care of *themselves!*" she said, adding, "They need to take individual responsibility." Others in the group chimed in to affirm her perspective. The conversation went on like this for a while and I tried to listen deeply to what was being said.

I finally interrupted the discussion and said that I was puzzled. When I hear "personal responsibility," I think of individualism...every person for his or herself. But they had spent the whole first part of this conversation—forty-five minutes—talking about all the ways they help each other out. What did they mean?

This stopped everyone in their tracks!

We proceeded to explore all this further. The idea emerged that in talking about the ways they help each other out they had been referring to "communal duty." In their community, they saw themselves as having a duty to each other. They saw federal programs as interfering with this duty—even though the needs were so great that they would never be able to meet them all themselves. They also found it disturbing that it was against the law to share your electronic SNAP food benefits with people outside your household. They thought that this was undermining their sense of communal responsibility. I was stunned.

After returning home I reflected on the group session. I believe that among participants there may have been some shame driving their anger at SNAP recipients for not taking care of themselves. But also, community members were ashamed that they could not take care of the needs of everyone in their community. Such shame can lead to the protective coat of anger and judgment. What a challenge.

Listening deeply, without judgment and without giving in to the impulse to advocate for my own position, brought me to deeper understanding. Just showing up, with curiosity and humility and with no predetermined sense of the "right" answer, led to new insight. In my experience, the practice of contemplation has expanded my capacity to do this.

Contemplative practice has enabled me to stay open and avoid a defensive, knee-jerk response when I hear things that challenge my own ways of thinking. Rooted in contemplative practice, I was able to help our group break through some of the partisan rhetoric and explore what we actually mean by being in relationship with each other. This is a direct benefit of a meditation practice that is not about judgment but is about inclusion.

My experience of meditation hones my curiosity to understand the other. It reduces my fear of exploring something with which I might disagree. It causes me, on good days, to listen to the underlying messages and feelings. And, in the end, it brings a deeper understanding of those I encounter.

It is this experience of deep listening that opens me to the needs of others in our nation and in our world. It is also a practice that can sometimes weave us together more closely with new insights, thus providing an anchor of hope in a turbulent world.

QUESTIONS FOR REFLECTION

How do I experience listening with compassion?

When have I heard the "still, small voice"?

To whom do I listen?

How do I exhibit curiosity about people who think differently?

How can I find understanding?

In what ways do I make judgments about people I do not know?

What can I do to move beyond these judgments?

3

Sensing the Divine

Listening to the "wee small voice" has led me to know that we are all connected. St. Paul is correct when he says that we are one body (cf. 1 Cor 12:12–27).

Some years ago after completing seven weeks of Christian/Zen renewal in the desert of Tucson, Arizona, I was feeling sad that my time there was almost finished. I said to the Divine, "O God, I am going to miss you in these mountains!"

My emphasis was on place.

The response was immediate. What reverberated across the landscape and in my being was "NO, SIMONE! I AM *everywhere*."

In that moment, I truly knew that God creates us and all of creation at every moment. God "hums" us at every moment. Sometimes, we are not aware of the Divine because the Divine is so close. But in stillness, I have discovered that God not only "hums" us but that there is a vibrating divine energy at the heart of all creation.

DIVINE IN THE CHAOS

In the current political chaos, it is of critical importance to allow ourselves to experience a contemplative moment, to remember that at the core of all creation is the loving, creative presence of the Divine.

The contemplative moment has been described by a variety of authors as "taking a long, loving look at the real." In my experience, this means slowing down and savoring the profound reality of a loving Creator who holds us together at every moment. I love being on retreat in a picturesque place. I love being in the mountains or at the beach. I sit still and marvel at creation vibrantly alive, being "hummed" by the Divine at every moment. At such times, creation and beauty renew me. In the silence, I experience fullness and awe.

However, in my daily life I have discovered that this looking with love at the real comes with a cost. I have come to see that it is not only my friends and the people with whom I agree who are created in love and whom I am called to love. If the Divine is creating all creation at every moment, then the Divine is also creating people with whom I disagree.

When pushed to this insight, I realized that I had a mental—and unacknowledged—"mistake of God" list. On this list were people like Congressman Paul Ryan, Senate Majority Leader Mitch McConnell, and President Donald Trump, who currently tops the list.

What do I do with the profound truth that I viscerally disagree with these people and their policies and yet am called to love them? I will not claim that I am good at this, but I do know that the only way to move toward bridging the huge divides in our country is to be able to hold an open heart for those I see as political opponents.

LOVING AND CHALLENGING

At the prayers of the faithful during a liturgy on my last retreat, I prayed out loud for the current administration in Washington, DC. Then I began to cry quietly. I felt so powerless in confronting the horror that this administration is creating. I felt so small in the face of the white supremacy the administration is supporting. I felt powerless as it terrorizes children and families. I felt angry as it defiles the earth and undermines the basic dignity of so many.

How can I "radically accept" the president and his administration when they are doing so much harm?

I do not have a clear answer. What I do know is that all creation is based in love and part of a harmony bigger than we can ever fathom. I also need to place the president and the members of his administration in my care—hold a heart for them—even in light of what they are doing. But, faced with the human fear, hate, anger, and violence that they promote, my temptation is to respond in kind.

The Christian call is to love our enemies. I find this extremely difficult, but what I am coming to realize is that loving is not acquiescing to their hatred and fear mongering. Rather, radical acceptance of the person requires encountering them in a way that they can see their best selves. It means speaking with compassion and courage when the temptation is to walk away, hold a separate protest, and not engage.

In advance of Pope Francis's visit to the United States in 2015, we themed our Nuns on the Bus trip: "Bridge the Divides; Transform Politics." One of the early stops on the trip was in Topeka, Kansas. We visited a homeless shelter that was overwhelmed because the state government had cut almost all funding for low-income families. The shelter was overflowing with people who were destitute. We then went to a local church to hold our town hall meeting. To my surprise, the Westborough Baptist Church was picketing us. The group is principally one extended family that has made its life's work that of picketing against the LGBTQ community, progressive faith perspectives, and anything else the church objects to. Church members become a disrupting influence by yelling hateful slogans.

When I discovered that they were present, I went across the street to talk with them and try to "bridge the divide." The teenagers were holding signs that stated: "God Hates." I began the conversation by introducing myself and saying that in scripture I had read that God is love. One of the teenagers started yelling at me, "Psalm five five!" I thought he was trying to tell me it was Psalm 55. Later, we figured out that he meant verse 5 from Psalm 5: "You hate all evildoers."

The venom coming from the adults and teens was toxic. I was unable to connect with them in any fashion. They just continued yelling. As I reflected on the experience, I realized that I should not have started with scripture! Catholics do not have the same resonance with the scriptures that the Baptists do. Rather, I should have started with the two adult men and asked if these were their children. I should have asked to be introduced to them. I don't know if this would have changed the conversation, but it would have started it in a more relational place. And it would have changed my heart.

Contemplative practice helps to ground me in the experience of the Divine as creating us at every moment. I have learned that, when I am insecure, I am more inclined to fight or get defensive. When I am grounded in the deep listening of contemplative practice, I have no need for fear . . . only a need to connect.

RADICAL ACCEPTANCE AND LOBBYING

While Congressman Paul Ryan was chair of the House Budget Committee and before he was Speaker of the House, I learned that radical acceptance meant caring about him too, even if I disagreed with his position on policy. For me, this was dramatically demonstrated the first time that I got to lobby him in person. It was just the two of us in the room, and he was busy "impressing" me with his knowledge of numbers in the budget and his style of politics. I was trying to hold a heart for him as well as my position in the policy fight.

During our conversation, he said that he "kept his family in Janesville, Wisconsin" and "slept on a cot in his office." I reacted with compassion. I asked him if this was good for him or his family. He appeared to be quite surprised that the "self-imposed sacrifices" that usually got him points with constituents had caused me to be concerned for him. In response, he quickly changed the subject. But in that moment, I learned the importance of holding a heart for the person I am lobbying. I believe too that it changed the nature of the relationship between us. For the next five years while he was in Congress, as I continued to lobby his office, he and I related not solely as adversaries but as human beings. We were people with strong and often differing views struggling to find the right answers in a context of mutual respect.

Maybe, if I had a chance to speak directly with the president, I could both present my position and care for him. When I consider the human being who is at the core of "Trumpism," I find a seriously flawed man. He has no trust of others and has no plan or interest in policy. It appears that he is interested only in destruction, chaos, and division. Radical acceptance does not accept his hate and fear mongering, or that of his followers, but it does accept the people underneath the hate. Only a contemplative practice, only glimpsing the Divine, can even make me think of such a proposition.

This prayer practice allows me to recognize that mystery is part of life. It allows me to accept that I am not in control—and that that is all right. Being comfortable with a vision that is not my own allows me to accept my small part in the human story and to accept that others have their part to play also. In short, this practice allows me to open up to a reality beyond my personal boundaries. In my experience, this is the Divine.

Radical acceptance, however, is not enough.

FIGHTING FOR A VISION

I was first exposed to the lesson of radical acceptance while on an annual retreat. A challenging practice during that retreat involved learning to hold a heart for those with whom I dramatically disagree (and want to vote off the island). Once I got to what I thought was a "holy place" of acceptance, my retreat director pushed me to engage the issue of fighting! I resisted. I objected. I complained. I thought that I had not heard him correctly. Fighting? He said that it seemed to him that I did a fair amount of fighting in Washington, DC. With that, he ended our conversation. He left me sputtering!

As I thought about it, I realized that in our political efforts I am often "fighting against" a proposal. How many times have I said that we should "push back" against an administration plan! Gradually I came to see that when I push back against a policy or a position, my action has a tendency to reinforce the very thing that I am trying to stop. Imagine one fist pushing against another fist. This can either stop both sides in a stalemate or result in triumph for one side or the other. I realized that, if we take a long and loving look at the real, then fighting against a vision will not work. Rather, we need to fight FOR a vision.

Being in advocacy means that we articulate the values and vision that we are fighting for along with the details of the legislation we are proposing. Immigration policy is one example. We talk about the inherent dignity of all people and each person's right to be treated with care and respect. This means that any policy must care for families, protect children, and honor our international agreements to provide asylum to those fleeing persecution.

Politicians and their staff often prefer that lobbyists provide statistics and numbers as we advocate for a policy. We need to have the data available, but data, I have found, has never changed a mind, a heart, or a policy position. Rather, what has made a difference in my experience are the stories of real people and an alternative vision. Storytelling is the most powerful tool to engage compassion and make change.

The first time I experienced the truth of this insight was during a lobbying meeting with Paul Ryan. We had been talking about his proposal to cut food programs for working poor families. He thought they did not need the economic support. I told him about a family I had met at St. Benedict the Moor Dining Room in Milwaukee, Wisconsin. Billy and his family ate at the free dining room most nights because he and his wife did not earn enough to pay for rent *and* food for their two growing boys. They used their food stamps (SNAP benefits) for the boys during the day. Billy told me that it was okay for parents to eat once or twice a day, but it was not okay for growing children.

When Congressman Ryan heard my story, his response was: "These people are not the target of my program." My response was: "They are going to be your victims."

In the end, his proposal did not pass Congress, and I learned an important lesson about holding a heart for the people I am lobbying as well as holding a vision of the world we seek.

Encountering Fire

When we combine radical acceptance with fighting for a vision, then the fire of Pentecost is released into our world. It is then that something new can happen and our wounded world can experience healing. I know that a consistent contemplative practice in the morning centers me, but what is more important is that it changes me throughout the day.

I was recently in Rome lobbying to get women religious the vote at a Vatican meeting on the Amazon region in South America. We had several press interviews. After one interview, I realized that I had been sitting with my hands in the prayer posture I use every morning, my right hand cupping my left and my thumbs lightly touching. The physical posture helped me stay in the listening space that allows for openness, clarity, and welcome.

When we are not in a "centered" space, we often respond reflexively to people who oppose our view. We "push back" and get stuck in the cycle. Only with a consistent, contemplative practice can we have the courage and discipline even to consider the concept of both "radical acceptance" and "fighting *for* a vision," much less acting on it.

I believe that these times call for all of us to listen deeply to the world around us and let the Divine flame up in our lives. Only the Spirit alive in our midst can breathe over this chaos and draw out a new creation.

Based on my own experience, I know that my advocacy and action in this world are the fruits of my contemplative practice. I believe that the Spirit is breathing through us and can use us in this creative and challenging moment to love beyond measure. This is the source of my joy.

A contemplative practice that is grounded in radical acceptance and fighting for a vision of the future is the only way I know that we can move forward. This combination is fire, like the burning bush in the Book of Exodus in the Hebrew Scriptures. We become the sacred place where the Divine flames up and tells us, "I have heard the cry of my people" (cf. Exod 3:7). Out of that sacred moment, we are sent to "pharaoh," to set our people free.

QUESTIONS FOR REFLECTION

What do I see when I take a "long, loving look at the real?"

Whom do I find difficult to radically accept? What people are on my "mistake of God" list?

What vision am I "fighting for"?

Where do I experience the burning bush? Where am I aware of the Divine being close?

Part II

The Community

Nurturing a Prophetic Imagination

Contemplative practice connects us to each other as one body. But how do we support this practice in such a turbulent world? Connection is very difficult when the dominant culture emphasizes individualism. Each day, I use my cellphone to post my tweets. I speak my truth, express my opinions. Each of these interactions underscores my individuality.

The gospel truth is that we are all connected. We are one body. Christ is the vine and we are the branches. The Gospel says we are judged by how we treat the most marginalized people in our world, but Western values say that we are judged by how much money, power, and fame we have accumulated individually.

The gospel truth challenges us to move away from endemic individualism and focus on community. In order to be effective, a community must find ways beyond the hyper-individualism of our time. It is difficult to imagine how this might be achieved. Certainly, the "deep listening" practice of contemplation nourishes me, but what can nourish *us*?

Scripture scholar Walter Brueggemann has studied the communal context of the prophets of the Hebrew Scriptures. In his book, *The Land: Place as Gift, Promise and Challenge in Biblical Faith,* he notes that in the chaos of their time those who spoke out against the status quo were rooted in community. Their insight and courage came from a community that supported them even when the existing power structure turned against them. Brueggemann concludes that a critique of the dominant culture requires being rooted in a community that can imagine beyond the social constraints of the time.

It is in community that courage is born and change is imagined. This is particularly the case in a time of political polarization and stalemate like our own. We need an imagination that can look at the anguish and chaos with fresh eyes and a new imagination. The old ways are not working. Something new needs to emerge. How can we "hunger and thirst" for justice sufficiently to create new ideas, new ways forward? We need a new vision, but how can we find it amid the media sound bites and swirling chaos?

In the preface to the second edition of *Prophetic Imagination*, Brueggemann identifies five community characteristics that nurture a prophetic imagination. They are: (1) a long and available memory, (2) touching the pain of the world as real, (3) having an active experience of hope, (4) effective discourse across generations (and I add cultures), and (5) the capacity to sustain long-term tension with the dominant culture. These five characteristics could be the anchor point of any grounded Christian community. They certainly ground my experience of religious life.

Women religious in the United States have been the center and source of much prophetic imagination. My sisters are not often cowed by the status quo. They have learned not to take prior structures as a determinant of the future reality. My sisters are faithful to the Gospel and to prayer. In my religious community, we often speak of being led. We are women on the move, with hearts wide open to respond to the needs of our time.

Brueggeman explains that each of the five characteristics he has listed draws us out of our individual mode of expression and toward a communal one. My experience is that a communal context for our lives can be the antidote to hyper-individualism. By relying on each other for insight and sharing our own perspectives, we can imagine and create a new reality.

Community does more than simply sustain us in our contemplative journey. Community allows us to imagine a new way forward. Amid economic domination by the few and the political chaos of our time, it is difficult to do more than grieve. In many of the groups in which I take a part, there is continuous lamentation: "Oh, woe is me!" becomes the refrain. Old strategies are not making a difference and the exploitation of our earth and our people continues. "Oh, woe is me!" Government is unresponsive to the needs of the marginalized people in society. In fact, the current federal government seems focused on undermining any governmental response to people's needs. "Oh, woe is me!" We need a new imagination to create a way forward in these unprecedented times. What is old is not working and something new needs to emerge.

Given the experience of the prophets in the Hebrew Scriptures, we can trust that, by being rooted in a community with these five characteristics, we can help create an innovative response to our times.

4

A Long and Available Memory

The first antidote to the hyper-individualism of our time is to nurture a long and available memory. When we focus on the individual self, we lose sight of our context. Without that context, we can easily drift along aimlessly, meaninglessly. Having a longer memory connects us to a context that makes us part of a broader story. This not only can be comforting but can also give us the jolt that we need for action.

MY FAMILY HISTORY

Having grown up in southern California with only a nuclear family, I have always been fascinated by the possibility of having deeper familial roots. Half-jokingly, I often claim that one of the reasons I entered my religious community was because I wanted a large family at the Thanksgiving table! Belonging and history have always been important to me.

After my mother died, my siblings and I found a thick book written by her father's cousin, Effie. It recounted her research into the history of all of the landowners in Prince George's County, Maryland, and other information that this eccentric cousin thought was important. The book is a self-published, poorly written work based on an exhaustive re-counting of data in the county archives . . . as well snippets from Cousin Effie's imagination.

As a Christmas present for my siblings that year, I searched through Effie's book and pulled out a summary of our maternal grandfather's relatives. In the process, I discovered that our great-great-great grandfather had been a member of the Maryland legislature! I am not sure why, but it was comforting to know that he and I shared a passion for and an interest in political action. The book also provided information about his gravesite and that of his wife as well as the gravesite of our great-grandfather. After Christmas my sister, her husband, and I went on a treasure hunt to see if we could find the gravesites and learn more about our ancestors' stories.

The oldest gravesite, out along the Piscataway Road east of Washington, DC, was where we found our great-great-great grandparents, who had died in 1857. Their graves were marked off from the rest of St. Mary's Parish Church Cemetery with a set of metal poles rising about a foot from the ground. Clearly, a person or persons had thought it important to give special recognition to the couple. Discovering this moved me deeply. Five generations ago another relative had cared about our political process and had engaged in the struggle for democracy.

The story, however, gets more complex. Further research revealed that my ancestors from the 1800s had been not only landowners but also slave owners. This also affected me deeply. It was painful to discover that these relatives, whom I at first had rejoiced in finding, also had a shameful side as active participants in the original sin of our nation.

This dual memory of joy and horror underscores the importance of history in creating a community that can nurture a prophetic imagination. Memory reveals both strengths and weaknesses. We are affected by both the good and the evil. The truth of history can bind us together and help us create a bigger imagination anchored in the truth … even when it is painful.

This example demonstrates how memory can help to shape us and provide a sense of rootedness. In our own time, many want to forget, or at least ignore, the importance of historical connections. To move forward, we need to own this complex truth. I am challenged to own the truth that I am the descendant of politically active people and slave owners. Who else might be in my family tree? If we are to heal the "sin-sick soul" of our nation in these challenging times, we need to learn from our individual and collective history.

The Importance of Saints

The anchor of memory also plays an important part in church history. When I was in seventh grade preparing for the sacrament of confirmation, we had to choose a "confirmation name," which involved doing a bit of research to select a saint we admired. In our classroom we had a book called *Lives of the Saints* that provided a short biography of a saint for every day of the year. While looking through the book I was quickly captivated by the story of St. Genevieve, the patroness of Paris, whose feast is celebrated on January 3.

According to the story, Genevieve protected the city of Paris against the Huns in the fifth century. While the leaders of Paris were cowering, she marched out of the city and confronted the invading hordes. She successfully saved her city and spread the Christian faith. Of course, this dramatic story appealed to my adolescent self. It stirred my imagination and impressed on me that women can confront challenges and be leaders. In choosing Genevieve as my patron, I felt that I, too, could make a difference by being committed to faith and justice.

SCRIPTURE AS HISTORY

Scripture can also be a source of learning in our time. For me, a treasured passage is the account of Jesus walking on the water. An important part of the story is that Jesus, after teaching all day, sent the disciples in a boat ahead of him. "After he had dismissed the crowds, he went up the mountain by himself to pray" (Matt 14:23). Note that Jesus also needed time alone for prayer and reflection away from the pressure of leadership and the questions of bewildered apostles. He needed to have a break from teaching the multitudes. What we learn from this is that, if we are going to follow in his footsteps, we need to follow his example and draw away at times.

After a time in prayer, Jesus sees the apostles' boat struggling through rough waves and a headwind. Jesus walks toward the boat. Seeing a figure walking toward them on the water, the apostles fear it is a ghost, but Jesus calls out to them, "Take heart, it is I; do not be afraid." Peter responds by saying "Lord, if it is you, command me to come to you on the water." Jesus says one word: "Come!"

Peter gets out of the boat and begins walking on the water toward Jesus. However, once he realizes that he is walking on the water, he panics and begins to sink. Jesus puts out his hand and rescues Peter and then chides the apostles for their little faith.

Peter is my patron saint, and this story resonates with me. Like Peter, I can be impetuous. I have been known to leap into situations and then have second thoughts. For me, this story demonstrates that in the face of "headwinds" faith can make all the difference.

COMMUNAL HISTORY

I recall an experience where this scripture passage gave me courage and inspired me to reach out in turbulent times.

A few weeks prior to the 2012 Democratic National Convention, I was invited to speak at the event. At the time, I was on vacation/retreat at the Taizé ecumenical monastery in France. Distance made it difficult both to negotiate with the Democratic National Committee and to confirm NETWORK leadership's agreement.

After several exchanges, NETWORK agreed that it was a good idea and the Democratic National Committee consented to my three requirements relating to what I would say. These were that I would: (1) lift up the stories of people at the margins whom I had met, (2) share that I was "pro-life," and (3) make clear that our efforts at NETWORK in helping to shape economic policy were intended to benefit

100 percent of the population. At this point, I thought that I had completed my part in the process.

However, like St. Peter, I had leapt out of the boat by leaving my religious community, the Sisters of Social Service, out of the process! I had never even thought of them because, in my community, we are expected to do whatever is needed to fulfill the job requirements of ministry. I focused on the work and not on the impact it would have on my sisters. My limited focus was on the opportunity and the needs of those I had met on our first bus trip. Consequently, I inadvertently left my own community's leadership out of my decision-making process.

I felt terrible when I learned that my sisters in leadership first heard that I was going to speak at the convention from the news media. This happened while I was returning from France. Apparently, the convention committee had been pressured into releasing the information.

My sisters in leadership were both surprised and nervous. Focusing on our years as an immigrant community in the United States, where we had worked more in religious institutions than in civil society, they saw the need to maintain relationships with a wide cross-section of people, including Republicans. Their legitimate concern was that my action could undermine a number of those relationships. Consequently, they thought that the decision to speak at the convention had not been a good one and asked me not to do it. I understood their position. It reflected concern for a complex set of relationships, including those with church leaders, as well as the need to care for the community. They had not arrived at their position lightly, but, I confess, I found their request very painful.

Nevertheless, I was reminded of the story of our own religious community. In 1920, our foundress, Sr. Margaret Slachta, was elected to be the first woman in the Hungarian Parliament. This was two years after Hungarian women won both the right to vote and the right to stand for election—such political action was at the heart of our charism!

Sr. Margaret had organized our whole community in Hungary to work for women's suffrage. The sisters and their lay colleagues worked with women across the country. The sisters also addressed the conditions of low-wage workers and championed the education of youth and many other social issues. We have a treasured photograph of Margaret in front of a statue of the Holy Trinity in the Castle District of Budapest near St. Matthias Church, where she was leading a large rally of women on one of the many social justice issues that she championed. She stood up and spoke out for all those who were marginalized in the very difficult times following World War I.

The memory captured in this photo provides an anchor for all of us as we enter the Sisters of Social Service. This memory has inspired our sisters over the decades in a variety of ways, and we are proud of our social activism. In Europe during World War II, our sisters were credited with saving over a thousand Jewish refugees. Through the 1950s and 1960s, our sisters in California were active in social service legislation. They led the organization of social workers and drafted key legislation. From the 1970s through to the 1990s, our sisters were involved in creating affordable housing in Los Angeles, serving on advisory boards for the regional Federal Reserve Bank based in San

Francisco. In short, we have always been active in federal and state policymaking.

This communal memory sustained me in the painful intersection of our community leadership's and my own assessments of where I was being called as a result of the invitation to speak at the Democratic National Convention in 2012.

Our assessments had disparate valid points, with "history" to support each side. But it was our communal history that helped us find the way forward.

What ensued was an email exchange with community members in which various perspectives aired. The result of the online conversation—dare I say argument—was an emerging communal consensus that supported the bold action of speaking. As one of my sisters said:

> As descendants of Margaret, we are called to this kind of courage. It is the center of our religious DNA. In a world where institutions at every level are failing people in their tenuous hold on survival, I believe that the world looks to us for this courage that questions, challenges and confronts while insisting all the while that there is room at the table for everyone. Nowhere is this witness more needed than in the political arena.

Reflections like these from my sisters grounded me in the needs of the time and lifted up our history as a religious community. While not fully resolving the different and important points of view, they did pave a way forward. In prayer, I realized that I needed to share not only my own story but also the stories of the people I had met along the way. History helped us to assess what truly mattered in the midst of a complex state of affairs.

Significant too was the knowledge of actual history and not just an idealized version of the past. Part of that history was the conflict and turmoil Margaret experienced in living out her vision of the Gospel. In reflecting on our current situation, it was important to recall that our history had also evolved in the context of complex and muddled realities.

Thus, anchored in the memory of our communal history, rooted in my own prayer practice, and trusting in the support of my sisters in leadership, even though they had a different view, I was able to speak at the Democratic National Convention. I spoke of the people we had met on our travels and how we needed to work for 100 percent of the population. I have since heard that the talk gave hope to many people across the country. It was the long and available memory of my community and the Christian scriptures that gave me the courage to speak from my heart about the needs of our time. This is how memory becomes an anchor for future action.

In this time of "fake news," we lose our footing. Without history, we become untethered from the struggles and insights as well as the mistakes and sins of the past. As Winston Churchill said in 1915: "Those who cannot remember the past are condemned to repeat it."

To be a community that can have a revitalized imagination to respond in our time, we need to be rooted in history. We need to understand the complexities of both then and now. We need to honor diverse viewpoints and, in the end, we must be present in that faith moment and respond to the call, "Come."

QUESTIONS FOR REFLECTION

What part of my family history helps sustain me?
What part challenges or embarrasses me?

What saint or person in history inspires or helps
sustain my commitment?

What scripture passage nourishes me in continuing
to engage in these turbulent times?

How do I deal with communal conflict?
When do I speak out? When am I silent?

5

The Real Pain of the World

Memory alone is not enough to create a community that can stir us and nourish a prophetic imagination. A second element involves touching the real pain of the world.

In a nation that spends billions of dollars every year to eliminate pain, this element is possibly the most counter-cultural of all. Nevertheless, letting our hearts be broken by the stories of those around us creates true community and connection.

For me, this is a fruit of contemplative practice. If we are truly all one and the Spirit of Love is at the heart of all creation, then the suffering of our time beckons us. By hearing the stories of those in pain around us, our hearts are broken open. When our hearts are open, we then have room for everyone. No one can be left out of our care.

Whenever I have risked letting my heart be broken open and listening deeply to the person I encounter, I have been changed and altered. This is part of the beauty of Nuns on the Bus, for I find that my heart is broken open every day that we are on the road.

By anchoring our advocacy in a broken heart, we create an urgency and honesty in the political process. Let me share two of the stories that have forever changed how I view our work in Washington.

A Failed Immigration Policy

A few years ago when we were in Missouri, I met a family of five children along with their elderly grandmother. There was sixteen-year-old Kathryn and her twelve-year-old sister, Stephanie, and their three young siblings. They were attending our rally at a church that served as both an educational and a service center for the immigrant community. Their story broke my heart.

Their parents, who were both employed full time, had gone to city hall to pay a parking ticket. This resulted in their being deported as undocumented persons. Despite the fact that the three youngest of their five children are U.S. citizens, the immigration authorities were not in the least interested in protecting them by delaying their parents' deportation.

Kathryn and Stephanie, who are also are undocumented, were brought to the United States as very young children and had no active memories of Mexico. The two girls were eligible for Deferred Action for Childhood Arrivals (DACA), a regulation established by the Obama administration to protect young people from being deported from the only country they really know. However, this eligibility for protected status gave no protection to their parents. It was small comfort for this family that the older children were not threatened with deportation.

Once the parents were deported, the five children were left in the care of their elderly grandmother. This frail senior citizen was totally overwhelmed by the situation. Kathryn tried to hold the family together by taking on many of the parental responsibilities while going to school and finding a part-time job. In the course of talking with the family at the rally, I learned that Stephanie, in her grief, had attempted suicide over the misguided idea that her family would be better off without her—such anguish, for a twelve-year-old even to think that her absence would be a gift to her family! While she was unsuccessful in her attempt, when we met her it was obvious to us that she was still seriously depressed. She wept quietly during our entire exchange.

After listening to Kathryn and her sister, my view of immigration policy was changed forever. Their story causes me to grieve for them and others like them, as well as for ourselves and for our nation with its dysfunctional immigration policy that hurts families and abuses children. While President Trump wants to demonize undocumented people, it is worth recalling Kathryn and Stephanie's parents, who, like so many other parents, work hard and care for their children. They are not demons. A broken heart causes me to speak up and not be silent in the face of the lies told both about immigrants and about our immigration policy. I leap from the safe boat and try to be faithful in speaking up for those who are the victims of our failed policies. For me, when my heart is broken open, it is like Jesus calling: "Come!"

HEALTH CARE

A broken heart weaves us together in unexpected ways. When we were doing our first Nuns on the Bus tour in 2012, we stopped in Cincinnati, Ohio. We were scheduled to be in an air-conditioned room that held about 50 people. However, 150 people showed up. In order to accommodate everyone, we held our evening event in the steamy outdoor parking lot. We didn't have chairs, but we were together and that was the most important thing.

Two women who attended the event that night, Jini and her partner Lynn, had come directly from Jini's sister Margaret's memorial service. They brought me a picture of Margaret, which I carry to this day, and they shared her story.

In the 2008 recession Margaret lost her job and, with it, her health insurance. Even though there was a history of colon cancer in her family, she was unable to get screening. By the time she was carried into the emergency room, she was terminally ill with the cancer. If the Affordable Care Act had been fully implemented when she lost her job, she would have been eligible for expanded Medicaid benefits and received the necessary screenings.

I remember hugging Jini, Lynn, and their nephew. We wept together and lamented this unnecessary death. I carry Margaret and her family with me as a sign of the urgency of getting health care to everyone in our nation. When I spoke at the Democratic National Convention that same year, I shared Margaret's story and said, "No more Margarets should die!" This is a pro-life stance.

But I did not tell this story just there. I have told it repeatedly so that legislators will wake up to the price that is being paid for their willful refusal to ensure universal access to health care. This is the painful truth of this family's experience, a truth that breaks open my heart.

Two years later, in 2014, while we were preparing for a rally in Lexington, Kentucky, a woman came up to me, put her hand on my shoulder, and said that she was one of Margaret's sisters and wanted to thank me for helping to heal their family. I was not paying full attention to her so, when she turned and walked away, I ran after her. I asked her to repeat what she had said. She told me again that she just wanted to thank me for having helped to heal her family. It turned out that she and her siblings had been arguing and blaming each other for Margaret's senseless death. In her story, I heard the guilt and grief of not having been able to intervene. My speaking of Margaret had helped make some sense of an otherwise senseless death.

This mirrors one of Jesus's experiences as recounted in Luke 7:11–17. He is on the way to the town of Nain when he encounters a funeral procession for the only son of a widowed mother. The widow's crying touches Jesus and he reaches out to comfort her. Touching her pain breaks Jesus's heart open to her need. He draws close to the mother and wants to act for her sake. His entering into her suffering leads to healing for her and life for her son.

When we let our hearts be broken open and weep together, we create a connection that has immeasurable power and promotes healing. In our day, we may not raise the dead person to life, but we can assuredly be instruments for raising broken relationships. When our hearts are broken open, we can be woven together in community, a community capable of creating healing and connections in these very turbulent times.

THE TEMPTATION

There is an important corollary to letting our hearts be broken open. To enter into the experience of pain, we must resist the temptation to "fix" the situation. If I am trying to fix the situation, then I am moving from my heart to my head. I think I can be in charge and have a plan. I do not really have to let my heart be broken because there is an alternative, a way out. I can handle this. The temptation in our Western culture is to think that we have the capacity to fix whatever pain we encounter. But this is not the case. By trying to fix whatever pain we encounter, we seek to be "in charge" and we seal ourselves off from the reality of the actual experience of others.

For example, at NETWORK we have been holding listening sessions in rural parts of the United States. As has often been mentioned, access to quality affordable health care is non-existent in many of these communities. Rather than allowing my heart to be broken open by the pain of a mother who talks about her fear of taking her injured son to a physician because her family has an insurance policy with a $5,000 deductible, I am quickly tempted to find solutions for this situation. Once I have moved into problem solving, I protect my heart from the sadness that lies at the heart of this mother's lived experience. This kind of "fixing" distances me from fully engaging the truth of the experience.

An obsession with fixing is also part of the political crisis in this post-2016 world. Very often, people from around the country email me urging me/us to *do something* to fix the awful trajectory that our nation and our world are on. This responsibility and the expectation associated with it weigh on our shoulders.

I have had numerous conversations with intelligent, influential folks in Washington and around the country. I have tried to set up conversations with people at the Trump White House. There is no one there who will respond. And, to be candid, if they did respond, I am not sure I would trust them. I have met with members of Congress and heads of various organizations. I have spoken with people impacted by the policies of the Trump administration. After all of these conversations, I am horrified by the magnitude of the damage being done to people and our civic institutions. My contemplative practice leads me to care for those who are creating this policy, but my practical, political self acknowledges the heartbreaking destruction and devastation the administration is inflicting on our people. I am not abandoning my mission to effect political change. Rather, I am letting the anguish of this moment break open my heart to the reality that there might be healing beyond my control.

WHERE IS YOUR BROTHER OR SISTER?

Perhaps one of the most challenging issues of our time has to do with immigration. During the Obama administration, we worked diligently to get Congress to pass comprehensive legislation that would address the needs both of undocumented immigrants and of businesses in our country. In 2013, we conducted an entire bus trip on the topic and put pressure on Republican senators to vote for the legislation. We were successful in getting an acceptable bill out of the Senate, but Speaker John Boehner refused to bring it up for a vote in the House of Representatives. Most frustrating for us was the fact that we knew we had the votes to pass the bill.

In the Trump administration, immigration has been the focus of much of the president's anger and even hate. He has created policies that tear children away from their parents. He has stigmatized people fleeing violence in their home countries and claimed that they are "criminals and rapists." He has locked up families and frightened whole segments of our society. We at NETWORK have struggled day and night to protect the interests of these most marginalized people. We have highlighted how U.S. policy in Central America is forcing the migration of so many. Our nation has militarized the police in Central America; created, through our trade policy, the opportunity for drug cartels to thrive; and turned a blind eye to the violence and persecution in the migrants' home countries.

These policies of the United States have created a nightmare for our immigrant brothers and sisters. Pope Francis often has spoken out about the anguish and the plight of immigrants internationally. His words are directly applicable to our reality in the United States. In a 2013 homily at the migrant island of Lampedusa, Italy, Pope Francis said:

> "Where is your brother?" His blood cries out to me, says the Lord. This is not a question directed to oth-

ers; it is a question directed to me, to you, to each of us. These brothers and sisters of ours were trying to escape difficult situations to find some serenity and peace; they were looking for a better place for themselves and their families, but instead they found death. How often do such people fail to find understanding, fail to find acceptance, fail to find solidarity? And their cry rises up to God! Once again I thank you, the people of Lampedusa, for your solidarity. I recently listened to one of these brothers of ours. Before arriving here, he and the others were at the mercy of traffickers, people who exploit the poverty of others, people who live off the misery of others. How much these people have suffered! Some of them never made it here.

The United States keeps inflicting pain on these brothers and sisters. We work for a legislative remedy. We sign on to amicus curiae briefs in the Court. We try to "fix" the problem. But we are too small in the face of such anger and hate.

The Ministry of Weeping

In June 2018 I went on a delegation with the American Federation of Teachers (AFT) and a group of faith leaders to El Paso, Texas. The plan was to hold a press conference outside the federal courthouse in El Paso where many immigration cases are heard. This was to be followed by a prayer vigil outside a children's detention facility in the Texas border town of Tornillo. I was to be a part of the prayer vigil and a supporter in the background at the press conference.

When we gathered outside the courthouse, I realized that in this building the law was being used for unjust purposes. I had gone to law school to practice justice and here the law was being used for injustice. I was overwhelmed by the pain I was witnessing and started to cry. I walked away to the back of the crowd to absorb this horror.

I then heard my name being called. Randi Weingarten, the president of AFT, wanted me to come and speak as part of the press conference. I worked my way to the front of the crowd. I had nothing prepared. I prayed, "Come Holy Spirit!" With tears streaming down my cheeks, I spoke briefly of the anguish created by the misuse of the law and presented a faithful patriotic alternative.

The response was powerful. I heard from some in our group and even from a couple of reporters that my tears had touched many. Their response led me to consider that, in this time of political horror, one of the ways we are called to respond is through a ministry of public weeping. This means not turning aside from the pain we see and experience. It also means not railing against those who cause this pain. Furthermore, it means embracing the pain and feeling it deeply. It does not appear that we can change this administration except through an election.

To create a community that nurtures a prophetic imagination, we must touch the pain of the world and weep together. This is letting our hearts be broken open. It is the only way that we can find a new way forward. There is no magic wand. There is no quick tactic that can shift the horror of this time. The only way forward is with a heart broken open and the truth telling that ensues. Maybe healing can happen only if we, like Jesus, are moved by a mother's tears.

QUESTIONS FOR REFLECTION

What pain of the world brings tears to my eyes?
Who has broken my heart?

How do I speak of this brokenness to others?

With whom do I weep?

6

Experiencing Hope

To have an active experience of hope might seem antithetical to touching the pain of the world as real. I have come to learn, however, that hope is present in the intimate exchange of the authentic stories of our lives. The two go together because, in touching the pain of the world as real, we are bound to each other in an intimacy of caring. Our hearts are broken open, and we let another person into our lives. It is this engagement that is the spark of hope.

SEEING THE SACRED

I experienced this intersection of pain and hope in 2012, on our first bus trip, when we stopped at the Padua Center in Toledo, Ohio. Sr. Virginia had created the center to serve the community. Their base was a century-old Catholic rectory in a shuttered parish. Ten-year-old twins, Matt and Mark, came on that Sunday morning and joined Sr. Virginia and others to tell us about their experience at the center. It was clear that Mark had taken on all the vulnerability for the two boys. He appeared shy and withdrawn, almost to the point of tears. Matt, on the other hand, approached us with confidence and welcomed us with a handshake.

The twins, who had been suspended from school for fighting with another boy, spoke about the altercation that had led them to this program. Apparently, another boy in the class had been picking on Mark, challenging him with words and taunts. Matt stepped in to protect his brother. One word led to another, and suddenly, the fight became physical. Matt was getting the worst of it when, to everyone's surprise, reticent Mark slugged the other boy. As a result of the melee, all three boys ended up being suspended from school.

Fortunately, Matt and Mark were referred to the Padua Center's program for youth. When Sr. Virginia and the staff did a home visit to explain their program and ask that the boys participate, they discovered that the twin's mother was bedridden with multiple sclerosis and diabetes. The twins were her primary caregivers.

The Padua team got medical care for the mom and wove the twins into their community. Matt and Mark broke open the hearts of the staff and expanded the community.

During our time there, Sr. Virginia asked if I wanted to see the place where the boys worked. Of course, though time was short, I wanted to see a piece of their world. Sr. Virginia explained that they had been raising capital funds to refurbish the hundred-year-old rectory. The third floor, which had been set aside for the youth program, was almost complete.

Matt and I raced up the stairs so that he could give me a tour in the brief time we had left before the bus had to be on the road. Matt showed me the computers that children were learning to use. He explained that he could not turn them on because their leader, Mr. T, was not there. Amazing discipline for an eager ten-year-old! He showed me their art on the wall and their gathering place. He then asked me: "Do you want to see something pretty?"

Of course I wanted to see what a ten-year-old thought was pretty. So I immediately said, "Yes!" Matt crossed the hall, opened a door, and flipped on the light. What was revealed was a newly refurbished bathroom with glistening tiles. These floor-to-ceiling white ceramic wall tiles had a blue fern pattern embossed on them. Matt, in awe, whispered, "Isn't it beautiful?" Then, reaching out his finger, he rubbed it over the blue fern pattern of the wall tile. He told me that I could touch it if I wanted. I immediately reached out my finger to feel the slightly raised edges of the ferns. In the process I touched this ten-year-old's sense of beauty.

At that moment, I knew hope—hope through the eyes of a ten-year-old boy, who saw beauty, cared for his mother, and loved his brother. I knew hope in a hundred-year-old abandoned rectory that was seeing new life and nourishing the community. I knew hope in the sacred moment of encounter. This became an anchor moment for me on our long bus trip.

When I was getting ready to speak at the Democratic National Convention, I wanted to include this story of hope in unexpected places. I thought that this insight might help all the political activists gathered in the hall and those watching on the television, because hope was in short supply—even in a campaign that often talked about it.

The people helping me prepare my speech said that it was too complicated and that I should not mention a bathroom from the podium. I took their advice, but I kept in the speech the story of the twins and their care for their mother. This part of the story gave me hope, although for me the most uplifting part was knowing that Matt had seen beauty and wanted to share it. The insight I gained from this has led me to ask other young people: "What do you see as beautiful?" Isn't this the essence of hope—beauty in unexpected places?

Being On the Bus

Over the years, I have come to realize that Nuns on the Bus is itself an experience of hope. Sometime between our 2013 and 2014 travels, someone suggested that we could have people sign the bus. What a great idea! After clearing it with the bus company that rents us the bus and making sure that black markers would not damage it, we created a "bus-signing ceremony" at the end of each of our stops.

Vice President Joe Biden was the first person to sign the bus in 2014, after the launch of our bus trip in Des Moines, Iowa. We were on the road for voter engagement and turning out the vote. The vice president wanted to support our effort. I had explained to him that we were going to have thousands of signatures on the bus by the time we finished, so maybe he would want to make his signature small.

Present at the ceremony for his signing were sisters on the bus as well as some members of the press who had gathered with their cameras. The spot where the vice president would sign the bus was flanked by flags. Cameras started rolling as, in a brief ritual, the sisters began to get off the bus and assemble. I handed the vice president the marker. He smiled and commenced signing with a big sweeping "J." Halfway through signing the next letter, a large curving "B," he suddenly paused, and, from the expression on his face, I could see that he had just remembered what I had suggested about a small signature. He leaned toward me and asked: "I didn't sign too big, did I?" I said it was fine (though it was not what I had expected).

His large signature turned out to be a gift. So many people wanted to "sign close" to his name. Some signed in the loop of the J or inside the top or bottom of the B. Others took pictures of their signatures with his. His signature became the anchor that wove many in our extended community together. In the course of that bus trip and during the ones that subsequently followed we collected thousands of signatures. I like to say that it is no longer Nuns on the Bus but all of us on the bus.

For me, this is the essence of hope. We know in the core of our being that we are connected. I belong "on the bus," and I belong to all those who have signed the bus. During our 2018 bus trip—Nuns on the Bus on the Road to Mar-a-Lago—we knew that there were many of our members who would not be able to make it to a bus event. Because of that, and because of our eagerness to weave people into the community, we sent out clear stickers and invited people to send back their signatures so that we could add them to the bus. When the bus arrived in DC, our team was ready with ladders to add more than a thousand stickers sent in by people from around the country who wanted to be sure that they were on the bus! All these people responded because they knew the truth that hope is rooted in community.

EMPATHY IN ACTION

Solidarity with each other is fueled by hearts that have been broken open. Hearts that are broken open are moved to compassion. Compassion has been defined as empathy that leads to action. It is in compassion that the seeds of hope can grow. Compassion is the shared view of wonder and worry. Can we marvel together at the gifts around us and share the worry that they are not evenly distributed?

Compassion is a critical component of contemplative practice, which, as we noted, reminds us that we are not alone. It is not just about me and mine. Rather, contemplative practice leads us to know that we are all connected. This connection, the fertile ground of compassion, requires that we open ourselves to the challenges of others. This is where the seeds of hope are nourished as long as we have others to tend the ground with us. However, a life of living compassion is not easy.

While practicing law in Oakland, I had several extremely difficult cases in which I was court appointed to represent youth caught up in family law custody battles. These particularly challenging cases created much anguish for me as I tried to provide for these youngsters while their parents were focused on their own needs and wants in their desire for "victory" over a former partner.

Finally, after the conclusion of several of these most difficult cases, I took some sabbatical time to refresh my spirit. I realized during this time that I had been with my "nose to the grindstone" for so long that I had lost sight of the bigger picture. My sabbatical became an opportunity to "look up." By looking up and seeing the bigger picture—relationships, elements of beauty, and how we are all connected in some fashion—I realized that this is where hope is found.

In these challenging times, it is often difficult for me to look up. I become fixated on the latest tweet, the latest act of violence, the latest degradation of humanity and creation. This obsession is generally rooted in my anger and sense of powerlessness. Focusing on narrow individual actions, I lose sight of the broader view.

In community, I find nourishment, rootedness, and reminders to look up: look up and see the beauty that is all around; look up and see that we are not alone in the struggle; look up and know that we are bound together in the desire to be faithful and create a shared future.

Hope is definitely a communal virtue and, to the extent that we are lacking in hope, we are lacking community. Living in community breaks open our hearts, lifts our spirits, and sets hope free in our troubled world.

QUESTIONS FOR REFLECTION

Where do I experience hope in my ordinary life?

To what communities do I belong?
Who are my people?

How do I express empathy in action?

7

Effective Discourse

A fourth characteristic of communal nurturing of a prophetic imagination is to have effective discourse across generations and cultures. In my experience, this is critical because we need to get outside of our own bubbles. In our highly individualistic society, we can easily assume that everyone has the same experiences we have, or that no one knows the challenges we face.

As I travel the country, I often hear older people lament the seeming absence of younger people at the gatherings. This happens even on our Nuns on the Bus trips, when the entire staff on the bus is made up of people in their twenties! I also hear critical comments about young people on their phones, with "tats," in relationships without marriage, and so on. On college campuses, I hear student enthusiasm for new movements, but also how the younger students view older people as judgmental. If we are going to move forward together, we need to find venues to talk to each other across the divides. This takes work.

COMMUNAL INCLUSION

One of the great gifts of being in a religious community is that we often live in multigenerational settings. I vividly remember one night when I was a young sister finishing my bachelor's degree. I had stayed up almost all night finishing my senior project and was at the kitchen table typing away when the oldest sister in the house came down to fix me a snack. She had woken up and was concerned that it was three o'clock in the morning and I was still typing away downstairs. Her care was even more nourishment than the snack she prepared. Both, however, were important for getting the job done. While this was not technically "discourse," it was a level of caring that bonded us.

A hallmark of being together in my religious community is that we try to understand each other's points of view and find a shared way forward. In our decision-making meetings, we spend time in silent meditation as well as in more structured prayer. We speak of our own perspectives and attempt to listen with open hearts.

We do this, at least in part, because my community follows the spirit of the Rule of St. Benedict. His admonition is that, when a big communal decision needs to be made, everyone should have a say. He advises starting with the youngest and proceeding up to the oldest, reasoning that by the time you get to the oldest person, what needs to be done will have become clear.

When I was the leader of my community and we followed this advice, the decisions regarding what needed to be done usually did become clear. In the process, I noticed that in voicing their opinions the younger members were often more willing to take risks and eager to be adventurous. More senior members sometimes advised caution or some tweak to the proposed plan, but they also picked up some of the spirit of adventure of the younger members.

For example, our sisters in Mexico were considering taking over a shelter for abused women at the request of the state. At the time, it was only the third shelter for victims of domestic violence in Mexico. Our younger members were enthusiastic and excited about the work. They knew women who needed this protection desperately. Our older sisters valued the mission but raised the concern of how the priests and bishops were going to deal with it. Often priests in Mexico, and elsewhere, had been trained to advise women to return to their husbands regardless of the circumstances. Our senior sisters knew the shelter was needed, but they were concerned about the cross-currents of church attitudes.

We eventually came to a shared understanding that we would take on the work and include the local archbishop in the project. We went to meet with him and he agreed to participate. Our sisters would educate the priests of the diocese about domestic violence and the needs of women and children. We took the energy of the young sisters, the insight of the older members, and created an effective strategy for meeting the needs of women in danger. If we had not had this conversation across generations, we would not have created together an effective plan to respond to a desperate situation.

It is the combination of mutual respect and a shared sense of purpose that helps a group find innovative ways forward.

CULTURAL DIVIDES

Discourse across generations is critical, but it is equally important to have discourse across cultural and racial divides.

This became apparent to me when I visited our sister community in Budapest, Hungary. The sisters were amazing in their warm hospitality and providing me with guided tours. Each day, a sister literally held my hand wherever we went as we toured the city, whether it was walking through the museum, strolling through a park, or visiting other sisters. One sister got me on an English-speaking tour bus by holding my hand and walking me to a seat on the bus after having introduced me to the driver. She then waved me off. When the bus returned at the end of the tour, another sister was there to hold my hand as we walked to our next site.

Toward the end of my weeklong visit, I had a chance to meet with the young sisters who were in temporary commitment. They were learning about religious life and discerning their place within it. Sister Iren was in charge of their program. I asked the young sisters if they helped shape the program as our young sisters do. They replied "Oh, no! Sister Iren knows what we need!"

As we puzzled over this difference together, I came to see the impact of being in a country with a centrally planned economy. It is the task of the leader to think through what is needed and assign tasks. If someone were to offer the leader a suggestion, the leader would be seen as not doing the job that he or she had been assigned. The suggestion would be seen as a criticism.

In that same context, we talked about hospitality. I explained that I found it a "little" difficult to be always with someone and to not make any decisions. I talked about hospitality in the United States and told them that we give visitors a key to the house and a map of the area. We present options by providing a list of places to visit and things to see. We will offer to go along, but not "crowd" the company.

After I had described this different style of hospitality, one of the young sisters asked: "But Simone, how would we know that you care?" I was dumbfounded. I sputtered something to the effect that they would know I cared because I had given them a key to the house, had offered to be with them, and had given them great flexibility. It dawned on me that "democratic hospitality" is very different from "centrally planned hospitality."

Racial Divides

In our nation during these challenging times, it is also important to have effective discourse across racial lines. We know that the Trump administration has been intensifying racial conflicts by demonizing immigrants and vilifying African Americans. He has sided with white nationalists and failed to bring our nation together. This approach fuels his "base," but such stoking of anger is tearing us apart.

In attempting to have effective discourse I have learned that the reality of white privilege often blinds me to the deeper story in the conversation. For example, when the issue of racism emerges, I am tempted to think individualistically and wonder, "Did I do something wrong?" In studying Robin DiAngelo's book, *White Fragility*, I came to realize that this individualistic response quickly shifts the focus of the conversation to me. This is a place of privilege, and it has nothing to do with genuine discourse.

Genuine discourse requires us to look beyond ourselves. In the case of racial divides, we are called to address the systemic approaches that have systematically excluded people of color from participating in our economy. Our study at NETWORK has found at least thirteen major pieces of legislation that, on their face, look racially neutral. However, the impact of these laws is that they have systematically excluded people of color from full participation in our growing economy.

The laws have to do with subjects ranging from slavery to "red lining" in low-income neighborhoods, where low- to moderate-income families could not buy property in certain neighborhoods because—legally—they were deemed to be "too risky" for the lenders. The GI Bill left out veterans of color, and so this group did not have the same opportunity as whites to develop a middle class in the post–World War II economy.

Much has been written about white privilege, but the challenge of this spiritual moment is to internalize the truth. We need to talk about it and lift it up in our communities— especially in white communities!

I have often found myself in settings where the white audience laments that there are no people of color in the gathering. In response to this, I try to point out to those gathered that the work of dismantling racism is principally white people's work. We need to understand the experience of people of color, but we need to dismantle our white privilege if we are going to make any real progress in atoning for the founding sin of our nation. Do not lament the absence of someone and use it as an excuse not to do the work. Rather, pick up the work and do it with those that are there.

Understanding Different Contexts

During our first few roundtable discussions in rural America, I was surprised that the issue of racism did not arise on its own. After the formal conversation ended, however, I would sometimes be approached by one or two participants who would say something along the lines of, "There is a problem of discrimination here." In one town where this happened, I asked what they meant. They answered that in this agricultural community there are many immigrant workers who have been in the community for more than ten of fifteen years, but the white people do not consider them "permanent residents," even though the agricultural community is dependent on them. The white community does not see the immigrants as adding to the local community population and sees no need to work on creating community with them.

This exchange taught me that I, or one of the participants, had to raise the issue of race directly if we were going to talk about it at all. In Michigan, one of the participants was an immigration attorney. She brought the subject up directly. Participants reflected on how the threats to immigrant workers created insecurity for the farmers. This insecurity "trickled down" to small business owners and schools. In short, the whole community was affected by the threat to the immigrant community.

In an African American town in the Mississippi delta, we had a conversation about education during which I learned about the almost complete segregation of schools in Mississippi—black children go to public schools, and white children go to private academies. Participants pointed out that the quality of education in both settings is at the bottom of the national ranking. However, the public schools are especially impoverished. Land values are low, and so the property taxes that fund the public schools are also low. Because of the scarcity of resources, the public schools are using the same textbooks that the students' parents and sometimes grandparents had used decades ago.

At the end of the gathering in Mississippi, I directly raised the issue of race relations. The first response was from a young African American woman back from university and working in her home community. She stated that children learn at an early age where they can go and what they can say. The participants added that, if you were in a neighborhood with sidewalks, you were in the white community. If you were in an area without sidewalks and with potholes in the street, you were in the black community. The matter-of-fact statement tore my heart, but it revealed a truth about race relations in the United States that I, as a white person, do not have to be aware of where I am. I assume that I can go anywhere.

My understanding was further expanded during a roundtable discussion that took place at the first gathering we held in New Mexico. We had been discussing the fact that there are large counties in the state without a single grocery store. I could hardly fathom this, and wondered how people could possibly shop without stores nearby.

Commenting with my "city culture" shorthand, I lamented that there were huge "food deserts!" One of the Pueblo elders chided me and said that I should not give deserts a bad name! The deserts are beautiful.

Later in the conversation, I commented on the extreme poverty in New Mexico. Again, a native elder scolded me, saying, "We are not poor! Look around at all of the beauty that surrounds us. We are rich in our environment. We just have an economic issue."

Moving out of my ordinary milieu taught me a couple of important lessons. First, I have a tendency to globalize the economic reality for the whole story of a family and a community. This is not accurate because the relationships in the community are their treasures and strength. Second, I learned that my "shorthand" to describe an economic situation can cause me to lose sight of other people's perspectives. I thought I was communicating clearly (and cleverly), only to discover that my shorthand was off-putting to people in other cultures, other contexts. I would never have understood this had I not had conversations outside of my ordinary comfort zones.

This reality is akin to the story of Jesus with the Samaritan woman at the well in the Gospel of Luke. As noted earlier, we are told that Jesus goes out of his native country of Israel into the territory of Samaria. Jesus is the immigrant, or some might say the stranger. A Jew was not supposed to talk to a Samaritan, and a man was not supposed to talk with a woman. Jesus was breaking all the rules. It was a moment of learning across culture and nationality. Jesus talks about the water of life that he will give. I find life-giving water when I move beyond my defined boundaries and cultural expectations. Jesus shows us how to break out into relationship that can nourish a new vision.

If we are going to create a faithful alternative to the political crisis of our time, we—especially white people—need to talk with candor about our privilege, open our eyes to the discrimination in our midst, and enter into authentic conversation across the various divides to create a different future for our nation. We need to be bold like Jesus and speak directly to those who are too often left out of our care.

QUESTIONS FOR REFLECTION

Do I talk to anyone from outside of my own generation? What have I learned in the conversation?

Do I talk to anyone from a different culture? What have I learned?

Do I talk to anyone who is of a different race from me? What have I learned?

How do I demonstrate that I am willing to learn from others?

8

Long-term Tension

The fifth—and possibly most annoying—characteristic of a community that can foster a prophetic imagintion is the capacity to sustain long-term tension with the dominant culture. This means recognizing that, no matter the community, no matter the institution, no matter the mission and goal, there will be tension if we are faithful.

When I was younger and decided to join my religious community, I sincerely thought that, if I gave my life to this call to justice, our world would be in a much better place than it is now. As time went by I gradually realized that my thinking had been unrealistic. When I expressed this lament, someone said to me, "Imagine how much worse off we would be if you had not given your life to this work." This brought me up short!

The comment helped me realize that the most challenging characteristic of a faithful community is the tension grounded in the reality that human beings will always have a flaw to be addressed. The basic flaw is that no one sees the whole picture or understands all of the forces and issues at play in any situation.

As the Navajo rug makers taught me, we need to live with the knowledge—the clear and certain truth—that each of our lives, like each rug, has a flaw that needs to be acknowledged and is embedded in the process. This flaw makes each of us unique and adds important depth to our lives, but it also is the source of our long-term tension.

Given this context and our very definition of our humanness, it should be no surprise that we never fully arrive at the "perfect plan."

Varied Perspectives

When the Affordable Care Act (ACA) finally passed in 2010, I was greatly relieved and delighted that health care was going to be extended to millions of people who had not had access before. I still rejoice in that success, but I have been continually amazed at efforts to undermine the legislation. Furthermore, the health care "industry" has continued repeatedly to seek ways to "maximize profits." This means charging people more money for the same service or medicine.

Thus, our "victory" was not the end of the story for which I had hoped. I had thought that we could move on to other issues. But, no! The dominant culture has figured out ways to sabotage the law for political gain as well as ways to bend it toward dominant corporate interests. The seesaw of interests is the norm, not the exception. It took me a while to realize this. At times, it has felt like a pitched battle against evil, but I have never met anyone who deliberately set out to do evil. Each person that I have met has had some explanation for his or her actions based on a particular perception of "the good."

This reality was underscored for me a few years ago when we were doing business roundtables to learn about the concerns of business leaders around the country. At NET-WORK, we felt that if we were really going to understand the dynamics of some of the political forces in the United States we needed to know what business required from and contributed to the common good. When we met with a group of top executives in Chicago, breaking news was that the average salary of a CEO of a publicly traded company was $10 million dollars a year, plus benefits. It was also reported that the goal for the following year was $11 million.

I asked this group of leaders if it was because they were not getting by on $10 million that they needed another million. I had thought that the only explanation could be "greed." The reply surprised me. They said that it was not about the money. I asked what could it possibly be about if not the money. They explained that they were very competitive and that they wanted to win. It just happened that the measure of winning was money.

What a revelation this was. Since then, I have reflected on the fact that I too am competitive. It makes me a good attorney (but a poor recreational game player). Certainly, we will not do away with the competitive streak that some of us have, but I wonder if we can change the measure of winning to something that has a less toxic effect than the growing income and wealth gap in our nation. I am not sure what the answer is, but I do know it is at the heart of the long-term tension with the established political reality.

What we work for at NETWORK is to bridge the economic chasm between the wealthy at the top of the income ladder and the 40 or 50 percent at the very bottom of that ladder. Dealing with the long-term tension does not mean shrugging our shoulders in a "ho-hum" attitude and just letting things be. No! We need to find a way to shift the economy so that it is more inclusive and thus benefit us all.

POLITICAL STRATEGY

A key aspect of the long-term tension with the dominant culture in the political setting is that we will never get the "perfect" legislation. In a democracy, there are always tradeoffs based on varied insights and experience. Pragmatically, we need to keep our focus on our chief goals and objectives and ensure that we achieve as many of them as possible.

This political approach can be challenging, and some of our activist colleagues in Washington occasionally regard it as a betrayal. There are times when I feel the "movement people" are unrealistic in their all-or-nothing demands. I get frustrated at campaigns for impossible asks. The long-term tension is thus not just with the broader society but often also with our own colleagues whom we think of as allies. I find it is contemplative prayer practice that helps me recognize the importance of this internal tension for the journey.

Some people in our community are able to move the conversation toward a vision that is bigger and more dramatic. Their vision of the world raises spirits, lifts imagination, and challenges the status quo. Such a vision creates more negotiation room for those of us who work in the realm of the actual. It is important to have inspirational headlines to move our societal imagination in a new direction. We are part of a drama that is bigger than all of us, and the challenge we face is twofold: first, we each need to know our role, our part; and second, we must remember that the play will never completely end.

POLITICAL TENSION

The toughest ongoing tension for me is the one that exists between our two political parties. Aside from differences in political opinion, Republican rhetoric stoking fear, hate, and violence creates even more fissures in our political discourse. The divisive and crass language of our day impedes the national conversation we need to have in order to create a democracy that works for the entire nation. It validates people like United States Senate majority leader Senator Mitch McConnell when they refuse to take up the very serious concerns of our time. The resulting inaction combined with a narrow vision of the role of government weighs on our nation and impairs our capacity to have a functioning government.

In this chaotic time, Republicans, if they say anything at all, only repeat the hateful statements from the Trump White House. They are frightened of a bully president who attacks anyone who disagrees with him. The extent of division and depth of fear are palpable. The Republicans' only policy agenda is to dismantle and destroy anything that President Obama achieved.

The Democrats keep focused on trying to improve the situation for struggling families in our country. However, they sometimes lash out in frustration.

In this situation, those who seek governmental change need to expand public awareness sufficiently to make the status quo politically uncomfortable for those who resist action. Those of us who seek change have to stay committed for the long haul, because we never know when the moment may finally come when even the "do nothing" legislators must act in order to survive.

TENSIONS AND FRUSTRATIONS

Political activism is like the image of the community as the body of Christ. We each have a different part to play. Sometimes seeing and acknowledging the various parts can be frustrating, because we want to have all of our friends with us in our part. That is not how it works. In the social process of nurturing a prophetic imagination, we have those who, like me, are in involved in negotiating policy options, trying to get as close as possible to actualizing the ideals we hold. We also have those who are staking out the "big vision." In some ways, we try to have it both ways: engaging politically at the practical level, but also trying to articulate a vision of an alternative economy that can work for all. At times, however, we forget what level we are working at, and frustrations can spill over, even with close allies.

We see this currently in sound bites such as "Medicare for All" and the "Green New Deal." These are headline-grabbing visions that create more space for moving policy ahead. But they are also shorthand for very complex ideas that need to be considered in detail and policies that need to be spelled out. We need the imagination to create an urgency for change and the capacity to imagine how things will look when that change has taken place. Both are critical if we are to create the space that can protect our people and our planet.

Problems arise when one visionary plan becomes the litmus test of how faithful a person is to some political idea or ideal. It is frustrating when television interviewers ask Democratic candidates if they support a particular visionary program and then criticize those who hold a different view. We need to create various possibilities that can move us forward so that the best ideas flourish. The process of doing this, even with colleagues who share the same goal, can produce internal tension and so presents a challenge.

To meet the challenge, I need to be rooted in a contemplative stance. In the Letter of James, the writer sets out the way of fidelity:

> But be doers of the word, and not merely hearers who deceive themselves. For if any are hearers of the word and not doers, they are like those who look at themselves in a mirror; for they look at themselves and, on going away, immediately forget what they were like. But those who look into the perfect law, the law of liberty, and persevere, being not hearers who forget but doers who act—they will be blessed in their doing. (Jas 1:22–25)

This is the core that nurtures fidelity for the long haul. Contemplative practice helps me to remain faithful in doing my part during this very challenging time. It gives me the sustenance to maintain a vision and commit to finding a way to a better future. It involves looking deeply and not forgetting.

The contemplative stance allows me to be an "equal opportunity annoyer." While we at NETWORK have stronger relationships with Democrats than with Republicans in Congress, we also lobby and push Democrats to get them to take up issues, shape legislation, and lobby their

Republican colleagues. Contemplative practice helps me stay focused on the goal of healing the income and wealth disparity in our nation. In many ways, it allows me to live the life of an outsider while working on the inside of federal legislation. Contemplative practice helps me seek a way forward for those who are too often passed over or left out.

The Dominant Culture of the Church

I understand and struggle with the notion of a "dominant culture" in national politics, but I am continuously surprised when it becomes evident in the context of the church. I confess that when it comes to the church, I am of the view that that our motivation and our focus should be the Gospel. However, I continually see in the institutional church the same political machinations that are playing out in Congress.

I spent a weekend with colleagues who are closely connected with the institutional Roman Catholic Church. There was much name-dropping, discussion of church political strategy, and downright religious institutional gossip. I was intrigued about a world I do not know, but also horrified that the Gospel has been so superseded by this very human hierarchical institution. The monarchical organization, rooted in the clericalism that Pope Francis laments, seems far removed from the Gospel.

Quite frankly, many times it just makes me want to weep!

My role is to work in secular politics and attempt to live the Gospel fully in the public square. This is the joy of being a woman religious in today's world. It is a vocation that connects my sisters and me with the struggling and most marginalized people in our nation and our world. We hear the stories of those who are most often left out of the news headlines and the concern of politicians. Because women religious and others are in relationship with people who are economically and socially marginalized in our world and church, we too become marginalized in the process by the institution of which we are a part. It is required.

As I read the Gospel, I see Jesus walking toward the religious leaders who judged him harshly. Jesus approached these leaders with questions, not condemnations. His story, and the accounts through the ages, make me realize that a community that can nurture a prophetic imagination in challenging times is one that is called to walk toward those who hold power but also ignore the marginalized persons in our community. We are called to walk toward those who promote laws that discriminate. We are called to walk toward those who disagree with us. In short, if we are to follow in the contemplative path of the Gospel, we are called to walk toward trouble.

SUMMARY

If we remember our history, touch the real pain of the world, have an active experience of hope, engage in effective discourse across generations and cultures, and can sustain long-term tension with the dominant culture, we will be able to be a community that cannot be silent in the face of injustice. We will be impelled to action. Like the apostles, we will be tossed out of the safe space of the upper room. We will be required to go out into the streets and bring good news to those who need it. We will be changed. The Spirit is alive in this moment, if we but listen to the still, small voice and respond.

This is the Pentecost we seek. This is knowing the Spirit. In knowing the Spirit, we walk toward trouble with hearts open to the stories of whomever we meet. In these challenging times, we cannot hold back. Rooted in contemplative practice, we must walk toward conflict and respond as we can. With confidence in the Spirit, we will not be left orphans. We will be given the words that we need. If we live in trust, then our community will support and sustain us. We will be the community that nurtures a prophetic imagination in challenging times.

QUESTIONS FOR REFLECTION

How do I handle being in tension with the dominant culture?

Am I angry that we will never "arrive"?
What sustains me in this tension?

What part of the body of Christ am I in this time?

What do I give to other parts of the body?

What do I need from other parts of the body?

Part III

Expressions of Hope

Contemplative practice and a community that nourishes a prophetic imagination are not goals in themselves. Rather, by participating in both community and contemplative practice, we are forever changed as they become the catalyst for our action in the world. From my Christian perspective, this is like Jesus sending the disciples out two by two. They are sent to make a difference, to preach a gospel of love. It is in this engagement that hope is nourished in our world.

Contemplative practice reveals not only the need for "deep listening" but also opens us to the complexity of life, which is much greater than I ever imagined. It has taught me that others do not share my view of the world or my experience. I call this general worldview the "wallpaper of my mind." As a young person, I did not know that others had different "wallpaper."

The first time that I encountered this difference was when I was in fourth grade. My dad had taken my sister Katy and me to an AAA baseball game. We had a favorite team and were excited to see them play. However, we had no idea that not everyone was rooting for our team. Somehow, many of the folks around us were not "with" us. My sister and I found this inexplicable. As we enthusiastically rooted for our team, we could not imagine how other people in the stands could be for the "enemy." My dad came home and told my mom that, because of the ruckus that Katy and I had caused, he would have to work out at the gym before taking us to a game again! We had had no idea that our being "clear" about our team would create conflict. But this incident introduced my sister and me to the fact that that people could see things differently.

Having discovered this, I went on to learn that there are various ways to respond. One approach is rigidly to insist on my own view. I have found that when I respond in such a manner, my rigidity is often based on my insecurity about the topic under consideration.

For example, when I was a young sister and we were going to renew our temporary commitment to the community, a big issue for us was the music we were going to use at the renewal liturgy. It was post–Vatican II and a "folk guitar mass" was what we young sisters wanted. The "tradition" was an elaborate ceremony with organ music and songs sung in Latin. They did not reflect who we were as young sisters in a post–Vatican II world.

We younger sisters met separately to prepare the talking points for "making our case" to the sisters in leadership.

The meeting we subsequently had with them was painful for all involved, because we young sisters were trying to change what the older sisters saw as sacred moments of initiation into our community. In the end, we found a compromise in a liturgy that reflected some of the old and some of the new. I recall singing the *Te Deum* in Latin at the end of the liturgy followed by a song from the musical *Godspell*. I detested the *Te Deum* and loved the song from *Godspell*. It was the reverse for our senior sisters. Nevertheless, while working out the details of the ceremony had been a difficult process, in the end, it was a joyous celebration.

On reflection, I came to see that the struggle had been fraught, in part, because of our youthful rigidity. Our insecurity about engaging our leadership made us more determined and more rigid. This, in turn, caused a firm reaction from our sisters in leadership. The final "negotiated settlement" restored a balance. It allowed the "wallpaper" of our celebration to be altered for us, but still recognizable to the senior sisters.

Now, many years later, when we gather as a community and are in the kitchen doing dishes, we often burst into song singing pre–Vatican II hymns with gusto. Our newer members seem to be learning them to "keep up." It seems ironic, but the fact is that the rigid old/new divisions have blurred as I/we have journeyed deeper into the spiritual life of the twenty-first century. We have recognized the treasure of diversity even if I would still choose a more informal style to celebrate my commitment.

An awareness of diversity is critical for the work of our time. When we must take action, diversity challenges us not to hold too tightly to our own interpretation of the data. Certainly, my prayer practice (and California upbringing) make this possible. My spiritual practice compels me to act, but it also compels me to understand a deeper complexity as we consider social issues.

Spiritual practice and growing maturity are at the heart of community, and community is the source of prophetic action. But, action itself and engagement with the complexity of our world create a tension and struggle. That tension requires that we stay engaged, listen deeply, and act on what we hear.

9

An Economy that Works for All

In 2010, all of us at NETWORK read the book *Spirit Level: Why Greater Equality Makes Societies Stronger* by British sociologists Richard Wilkinson and Kate Pickett, who studied ten measures from the United Nations that evaluate the quality of life in developed society. The authors examined these measures of quality in twenty-one developed nations and compared the results with the level of income disparity between the top and the bottom in each country. Their research question was: Is there a correlation between the quality of life and the income disparity? They considered issues of life expectancy, math and literacy, infant mortality, homicides, imprisonment, teenage births, trust, obesity, mental illness (including drug and alcohol addiction), and social mobility.

Their findings were startling. There is a direct correlation between the two. Quality of life increases as income inequality decreases. Even more shocking to us at NETWORK was that the United States has both the highest income inequality and the worst quality of life in the developed world.

Further investigation brought us to the realization that if we reduced the income and wealth disparity in the United States, quality of life would improve for everyone, even for those at the top of the economic ladder. This led to our study of income inequality and its causes. Our over-arching policy goal is to create a society where the entire population can live in dignity. To accomplish this, we must focus particularly on those who struggle with poverty in our affluent society. The statistics, we discovered, are daunting.

INCOME INEQUALITY

Our study revealed that between 1949 and 1979 income at every level of our society went up by about 100 percent. The bottom 20 percent increased by 116 percent, while the top 20 percent increased by 86 percent. Everyone was thriving in a post-war economy.

Between 1980 and 2016 the story is very different. In this thirty-six-year period, the income for the bottom 20 percent of households increased by 8.25 percent, while the income for the top 20 percent increased by 65 percent. This is a shocking variance. But it is even worse when you break out the top 20 percent and see what has happened to the in-come of the top 1 percent, which, in this same thirty-six-year period, increased by 205 percent!

These numbers and the reality they signify for our na-tion are horrific. Everywhere we have traveled, we have met struggling people who are living the reality of flat wages. It is not some boring graph; it is the struggle of real people.

In 2014, while we were in Chicago at a labor rights center, I met Lupe, who was an undocumented immigrant. For fourteen years she had worked at a year-round car wash in the city. Her salary was only the customers' tips that she made as someone who dried the cars. Her employer had told her that labor law in the United States did not apply to immigrants, so she had no grounds for complaint. Finally, a friend put her in touch with a legal center and the attorneys were able to get her back pay for four of the fourteen years. Because of the statute of limitations, they were not able to go back beyond that time. At least they got some justice for Lupe and her struggling family. The labor market was exploiting Lupe and all those like her.

How can such exploitation exist? In *Laudato Si'*, Pope Francis says that this exploitation can happen because employers, politicians, and other professionals "are far removed from the poor, with little direct contact with their problems . . . This can lead to a numbing of conscience" (no. 49).

Such exploitation of workers riles my heart. It is wrong and needs to stop. Pope Francis calls us to end an economy of exclusion. How did we get to this point? At NETWORK, we wondered about the drivers that had created the economy of exclusion that characterizes our nation today. How did we go from everyone benefiting from our economy to only the top 1 percent being the beneficiaries?

It is here that the contemplative life has a practical function. For, once again, it was contemplative practice that helped us recognize the connections that we might not have seen otherwise. As we traced the root of the problem, we kept returning to the policies of President Reagan in the 1980s.

THE MYTH

President Reagan changed the founding myth of our nation. The original story that I learned as a youngster in southern California was that we were founded in community, with the colonies in Jamestown, Plymouth Rock, Philadelphia, and other places. The colonies were composed of many people making a life in this "new world." Admittedly, absent from the original founding story was the impact on those people who were already here when the colonists arrived in the seventeenth and eighteenth centuries. The mythic narrative was about the European settlers struggling together for freedom of religion and self-determination.

President Reagan changed that myth, shifting it from the story of a community struggle to one of rugged individualism. The new story undermined the sense that prosperity was created by the community and was to be shared by all. It created instead a new myth, the false narrative of individual responsibility and "doing it on your own," a narraive that was used to fuel political gain.

POLICIES PROMOTING (OR MASKING) INEQUALITY

Tax Policy
The realization of the change in our nation's foundational story led us to discover a variety of federal policies that had contributed to the income gap. The first and most important was the tax policy promoted by the Reagan administration. The tax rate for the top income bracket in the 1970s

was 80 percent. This policy was a remnant from the Great Depression and World War II, when federal revenue was critically needed to pay for the recovery from the Depression and then the war effort. Because the highest earners were paying 80 percent of their top-bracket amount of income in taxes and keeping only 20 percent in after-tax dollars, there was not much incentive to get a higher salary because it was only going to be taxed.

The Reagan administration—with its strong emphasis on individualism—promoted the idea that the government should "return money to the taxpayer." Taxpayers "knew better how to spend their money than the government did." This led to the slashing of the top tax rate from 80 percent to 50 percent and then to 33 percent. Cutting tax revenue that dramatically undermined the various programs that had been established in the 1960s and were successfully addressing issues related to poverty in our nation.

The new tax policy also fueled the shift in corporate responsibility from being about the employees, the customers, and the whole community to being only about returning revenue to shareholders. This contributed significantly to the concept, mentioned in the previous chapter, that "money is the measure of winning," a concept that affects everyone in our nation and creates a situation whereby only those at the top "win."

Unions and Collective Bargaining

Through the narrative of individualism, President Reagan undermined the confidence workers had in unions and weakened the unions' ability to negotiate as effective advocates for workers.

Workers were told that they could not trust union leaders. At the time, there had been some stories about the very human failings of union leaders: some had stolen money from pension funds; others were no longer connected to rank-and-file members; and still others were living high and glamorous lives. President Reagan and his administration portrayed these failings as a problem of the unions, not as a problem of the human species.

At the same time, there were corporate CEOs who were guilty of the same kinds of failings, yet the political rhetoric did not focus on them. Instead, all the attention was shifted to the unions.

Finally, the 1981 Air Traffic Controllers' strike brought everything to a head. The administration ended up firing more than eleven thousand members of the union and in so doing broke its power. The long-term consequence of this action contributed to the disabling of the collective bargaining power of all the unions in this country.

Without effective collective bargaining, workers' wages have been flat for decades. As individuals, workers do not have enough clout to negotiate a just salary. By focusing on individualism and the untrustworthiness of the unions, the administration lessened their power to demand higher wages.

The impact was not just on wages. Unions' inability to engage in effective collective bargaining undermined their ability to negotiate for improved benefit packages for health care, vacation, paid family leave, decent working conditions, and so forth. Because workers in union shops were unable to get these benefits, non-union shops did not have to offer them in order to compete with employers who had workers in unions. This resulted in severe downward pressure on salaries.

Two-worker Households

Families adopted various strategies to deal with the issue of flat wages. One common strategy was to have a second adult in the household go to work. My mother, for example, returned to teaching during this time to help support our family. Having a second income helped cover up the fact that the primary earner had not received a raise for some time.

As stagnation continued, other strategies had to be utilized. There has been the increase of people working more than one job at a time. During the Obama administration, the president decided to phase in a raise for federal contract workers to $12 per hour from $7.25 per hour. As advocates, we championed this significant raise.

When I spoke with Connie, one of the workers at Union Station, she informed me that she and her husband were going to get a partial raise immediately and then receive increases over the next two years until they reached the $12 per hour minimum. I asked her how this was going to affect her and her husband. She said that she was excited by this very good news because her husband could give up his third job and spend more time with the family.

It turned out that Connie lived with her husband and young son in a small one-bedroom apartment in an economically challenged part of town. Her husband's mother also lived with them and provided childcare for their son. Both Connie and her husband worked a morning shift at Union Station and an afternoon shift at another site. Her husband also worked weekends at a third job, which he could now give up and so have weekends at home.

Credit Cards

A strategy used by the Reagan administration to mask the flatness of wages was to extend credit cards to just about everyone. They became the "safety net" for emergency expenditures. Credit cards masked the fact that working families did not have savings for unexpected bills. They also gave enormous power to the financial services industry, which has reached out to and taken advantage of unwary purchasers. As a result, some families now have high credit card balances that they are not able to reduce because they can afford to pay only the interest; they will never get out of debt.

In 2015, I met Andrea at an IHOP restaurant near Seattle University. She managed the "front of the house" on the early shift. I was curious about her experience of Seattle's recent increase in the minimum wage from $9.47 an hour to $11 an hour. Andrea is a mother of two middle school boys. She readily agreed that getting a raise had been an important benefit for her family. She said that she could now pay her regular bills and this eased her stress immensely. However, she still did not have any savings for unexpected expenditures.

She told me that one of her sons had needed dental work after being hit in the mouth with a ball during recess at school. She did not have the money to pay this large dental bill. I asked her if she put the charge on a credit card. She quickly said, "Oh, no! I'm not getting into that trap again!" It had taken years for her to pay off a credit card bill and she did not want to get stuck doing that again. In addition, the credit card balance was included in her credit report, which made it more difficult for her to rent an apartment and pay the increased the security deposit that landlords demanded.

I asked her how she had dealt with the dentist's bill. She told me that, although she didn't like doing it, she had taken their most valuable asset, a computer, to the pawn shop. She did it reluctantly, but felt that it was the most responsible way to raise the money without getting caught in long-term misery. This was her strategy to raise the needed cash without incurring additional debt.

RESPONSE TO INEQUALITY

Pope Francis makes it clear that excessive income and wealth disparity in our world are sinful. He points out that the poor have a claim on the goods of the earth in order to live in dignity. When those who are marginalized do not have sufficient revenue and resources, we have an obligation to change the structures that are creating the inequality.

For this reason, NETWORK aims to mend the gaps in income and wealth disparity. We are doing this by trying to change tax policy, raise wages, and provide benefits for workers through paid family leave. We are also working to make sure that everyone's voice in our democracy is heard by ensuring that everyone is included in the census and that all citizens have the right to vote. Health care and a right to housing are two additional elements of living a dignified life.

Finally, our immigrant brothers and sisters in the United States have a right to have their status acknowledged. Our immigration laws have not kept up with either the reality or the needs of our times. Immigrants who have been in the United States for decades have no status. They are exploited in the workplace and live in fear of deportation. In response, we must get our elected representatives to fix this very broken system to ensure that all those who work in our economy, worship in our churches, and attend our schools are treated with the dignity they deserve. By mending the gaps in our immigration policy, we will bolster our community.

RECLAIMING COMMUNITY

Policies alone are not enough. Contemplative prayer will make clear to us that we need to reclaim the founding narrative of our nation. We need to return to the true story—that we are founded in community and that it is community that will save our democracy. This founding story is not just a return to the idealized very "white" version of the founding of our nation. Rather, if we are honest, we must acknowledge the sins of slavery and the betrayal of the indigenous people that have cast a long shadow on our history. This is required if we are to embrace the full and complicated story of our community and become a people that "hungers and thirsts for justice."

Recently, in talking to someone, I stated my belief that everyone should have access to quality, affordable, and equitable health care. The person with whom I was speaking responded by saying that this was excessive and unnecessary. He then hurled what he thought was the closing remark, saying, "You are nothing but a socialist!"

20

Pont Poster
camerateur

My response was to laugh and assure him that this was not the case. I went on to explain that I was a "constitutionalist," that I believe in "We the People," and I invited him to join us. This belief is at the heart of the renewal of our heritage, and it is at the heart of contemplative practice.

QUESTIONS FOR REFLECTION

How do income and wealth disparity affect me?

What is my measure of "winning"?

How do I regard those at the top and bottom of the income and wealth ladder?

What do I do to further the common good?

Am I a "constitutionalist"?

10

Dignity for All

Over the past twenty years, I have come to regret some of my actions during the 1980s, especially some that involved my silence. Let me explain.

In 1973, in the case of *Roe* v. *Wade*, the United States Supreme Court ruled that a woman had a constitutionally protected right to choose to have an abortion. This set up a series of political actions that have been documented elsewhere.

The result was that the Republican Party became the staunch opponent of abortion while the Democratic Party became the party supporting women's options. The Republicans created a strategy to woo the Catholic hierarchy and the Evangelicals to their side. During the Reagan presidency, Republican leaders dangled in front of the Catholic bishops the possibility of White House meetings and other inroads into political power. Opposing sides in the abortion debate came to be characterized in the now-dated shorthand of "faith is pro-life" and "secularists are pro-choice."

At the time, as a person of faith, I did not want to identify with an ultra-harsh position that sought to criminalize

abortion. It did not connect with my experience. I was practicing law and had too many women clients who depended
on Planned Parenthood for various gynecological services
and treatment. A few of my clients had had abortions. They
had taught me that the banner headlines and the right-wing
rhetoric did not correspond to their experience. I knew that
their reality was much more complex than the sound bites
that drove the news cycles. I did not want to be identified
with what I considered to be the "far right."

Therefore, I made a choice that I now regret. Rather
than wading into the struggle and lifting up the nuance
of reality, I decided not to talk about a more complex—
progressive—faith perspective. I decided simply to live my
faith in action. I practiced law and served those who did not
qualify for free legal service and could not afford private
counsel. I did not use my title of "Sister" in the practice, but
all the judges and my fellow attorneys knew I was a sister.
And so it was that I, along with others, ceded the faith conversation solely to the anti-abortion campaign.

All these years later, the sides are still entrenched in polarized positions. Neither side has done the hard work of
finding a solution to the political stalemate. And no efforts
to create a shared way forward have gained traction because both sides deeply mistrust each other, see their opponents as monolithic, and use this as a lightning-rod issue to
galvanize supporters and raise money.

A Complex World

How do we proceed? I firmly believe that all creation has
inherent dignity because all creation is created at every

moment by the Divine. This awareness of inherent dignity is part of Catholic teaching, although that teaching does not require a specific political response, such as the criminalization of abortion. Nevertheless, some think that church teaching has only one political option. This is not true.

I am old enough to have heard whispered stories of desperate women seeking "back alley" abortions before the procedure was legalized. Many of these women experienced trauma, medical complications, and some even died. This tells me that desperate women will do their best to take care of their families even while risking their own lives. They have dignity and are made in the image of the Divine. The polarized conversation does not address their needs or the true complexity of their reality.

This was brought home to me when I was appointed by the court to represent a thirteen-year-old, eighth-grade girl in a family law custody proceeding. We will call her Jill. When I first met Jill, she was pregnant. Jill's family had earlier lost their house and found temporary shelter with her father's brother and his wife. While Jill's family was living with them, her uncle seduced and raped her. She eventually realized that she was pregnant, but she was terrified of telling her parents because her uncle had threatened that, if she said anything, her whole family would have to leave his house and they would be homeless.

When Jill finally told her mother, there was an explosive argument. The neighbors called the police because the altercation had spilled out onto the street. Jill's parents blamed each other and Jill. It did not appear that anyone, other than the district attorney, blamed the uncle. When the parents brought their divorce case to family court, the judge appointed me to represent Jill's best interests.

By the time I met the family, the parents had separated. Jill's mother blamed her husband for his brother's actions and also blamed Jill for breaking up the family. The father continued living with his brother and sister-in-law, while the mother, Jill, and her sibling scrambled to find new housing.

In my meetings with Jill we discussed her pregnancy. I quickly realized that there was no easy solution for her. As we reviewed her options, it was clear that this youngster was hungry for love and had some hope that her own baby could give her that love. The rape had traumatized her. Jill could not understand how her uncle, who was always telling her that he loved her, could have been so violent with her. She was dazed by what was happening and upset by her family's anger at her. She found it difficult to consider her choices.

None of the simple sound bites about "pro-life" or "pro-choice" worked in this setting. I prayed for wisdom, consulted various people I respected, and talked at length with Jill. It was an excruciatingly difficult time. In order to respect Jill's human dignity, I needed to embrace without judgment the pain she was experiencing regarding what to do about her pregnancy.

Jill ended up by making a choice, and I supported her in that choice. I do not know what has happened to her over the years, or how the choice she made impacted her. But I do know that I was forever changed by the experience.

What it taught me was that in the complexity of life, faith calls us to engage in a more nuanced conversation about what seem to be "dogmatic" principles. How we support the dignity of all life is a core challenge of the twenty-first century. What the polarized debate about pregnancy and abortion misses is that there are two lives that require the affirmation of their dignity.

Even after this experience, however, I did not voice my perspective publicly. I did not want to brave the ire of either side. I thought I could just keep my head down and continue in my individualism without engaging in the communal conversation.

DEEPER TRUTHS

As I have become more involved in the political realm, I have realized that my silence was a mistake. I have become bolder. I have learned to look beyond the rhetoric and more closely at the details of the "abortion reality." Ironically, prior to the full implementation of the Affordable Care Act, the abortion rate had increased during Republican presidential administrations, even though these Republican administrations had placed restrictions on access to abortion services. During Democratic administrations, however, the abortion rate decreased. At first, this seemed very puzzling.

Clarification came as a result of studies indicating that the chief driver of abortion is the economic circumstances of the mother. If a pregnant woman has access to health care and financial support to carry a baby to term, she is more likely to do so. It was reported in 2019 that, in 2018, abortions were at their lowest rate in decades. This was the first time that the number of abortions decreased in a Republican administration. The reason for the decrease was the Affordable Care Act's mandate that contraception be almost universally available to women who have some health insurance coverage. While this reduction in abortion is good news, far too many women still choose abortion because of their economic circumstances.

In recent years, the majority of women choosing abortion are low-income women of color. These same women are often judged harshly by those opposing abortion. Cherise Scott, the African American founder of Sister Reach, a reproductive justice organization, spoke in front of the Tennessee legislature. She spoke powerfully against the hypocrisy of the "pro-life" Tennessee state senators. Reflecting on her testimony, she says:

> As a Black woman of Christian faith who is uncomfortable with the weaponized mockery of Jesus, I ...called out the un-American and un-Christian hypocrisy of these self-identified evangelical politicians. I said: Many of you who claim to be conservative and Christian have weaponized the word of God to forward your political agenda and maintain power and control over the most vulnerable Tennesseans. You've manipulated biblical scripture to align with your colonialist, supremacist ideologies, instead of showing mercy.

She was correct in her ire and her accusation. How can we find a way forward together in mercy? With economics at the heart of the pressure for women to choose an abortion, it appears that the most pro-active way to support life is to ensure that women have a livable wage and access to health care.

It needs to be noted that, between the extremes, there are faith groups and faith-friendly groups that have focused on supporting women, both in having an abortion or in seeing their pregnancy to term. These groups are pastoral and engaged with the reality of women's experience. They exercise compassion in helping women make what is often a life-altering decision.

The public media frequently uses extreme stances to fuel the conflict. Additionally, leaders on both sides fail (and sometimes just plain refuse) to communicate with each other. They are not willing to recognize the nuance on the other side. Maybe making peace requires "missionary work" in talking to leadership on both sides of the debate. If we want to solve this seemingly intractable issue, we need some people to take on this work. We need to get beyond strategies for building movements and organizations and create strategies for caring for women and their families. However, it appears that, left to their own devices, neither polarized side of the abortion debate wants to find a settlement.

Rather than working on the extremes of this painful dilemma, I have tried to provide women with the economic and health care supports that they need to carry their babies to term. I believe that this is a more effective way to promote life. In our efforts on the Affordable Care Act, we worked with Senator Bob Casey's office to include an amendment called the Pregnant Women Support Act. It was authorization and funding for innovative programs to support pregnant women in carrying their babies to term. The amendment also provided for a five-year study of best practices to support pregnant women. This study is scheduled to be finalized in 2020, and the results should be available in 2022 or 2023.

Finally, and what has been most challenging, I have begun speaking publicly about this more nuanced approach as a faithful way forward. It has resulted in some hate mail and threats, but I find that my conscience is at peace. I have also discovered that many people in our nation share my concern for the articulation of a more complex, nuanced resolution. Many experience anguish in this painful debate.

Surprisingly at this moment in our history, my more nuanced view is supported by the writings of Pope Francis. In his Exhortation on Holiness, Pope Francis writes:

> Our defense of the innocent unborn, for example, needs to be clear, firm and passionate, for at stake is the dignity of a human life...Equally sacred, however, are the lives of the poor, those already born, the destitute, the abandoned and the underprivileged, the vulnerable infirm and elderly exposed to covert euthanasia, the victims of human trafficking, new forms of slavery, and every form of rejection. We cannot uphold an ideal of holiness that would ignore injustice in a world where some revel, spend with abandon and live only for the latest consumer goods, even as others look on from afar, living their entire lives in abject poverty. (No. 101)

Pope Francis's holistic view eases my heart and challenges me to explore further areas that undermine the dignity of life. My efforts in these areas have included work on economic justice, expansion of health care to all as a right, immigration reform, and a panoply of other policies. This is the healing agenda that can promote the dignity of all life.

COVERT EUTHANASIA

As I prayed over Pope Francis's words, one phrase puzzled me. I was mystified by the pope's use of the phrase "covert

119

euthanasia." I wondered what his words meant for people in the United States. Following some meditation, it became clear that for our country, Pope Francis was referring to the effort to undermine Medicaid and health care in general for the elderly and infirm. Many of our Republican "pro-life" politicians oppose health care for those living in poverty. These anti–health care policies undermine the health of our most vulnerable people and lead to premature death. Pope Francis makes clear that undermining health care is not a pro-life stance and is counter to the teachings of the Catholic Church.

Further meditation on this paragraph has led me to realize that human dignity needs to be protected on a societal as well as an individual level. In 2015, we started our Nuns on the Bus trip in St. Louis, Missouri. I met a woman who told me that, in her neighborhood, she and her family live near the Westfield Toxic Waste Site. When they purchased their home for a reasonable price, neither the realtors nor the seller told them that the house was in the area of a super-fund site that was scheduled to be "cleaned." The radioactive waste was left over from World War II work on an atomic bomb. She and her family discovered this the hard way.

A few years after living in this area, her seven-year-old developed a rare brain cancer. This was traumatic for the family. As she sat for many hours in the waiting rooms of pediatric oncologists, she began to recognize a few people from her neighborhood. She and another woman teamed up to canvas the neighborhood to see how many families had children suffering from childhood cancers. They mapped the results, which indicated that the rate in their neighborhood was 350 to 400 times above that of the general population.

The women went on a campaign to draw attention to the plight of their children. In the process, they discovered that not only was the site toxic, but an "underground fire" ignited by intense radiation was moving toward the Missouri River.

Horrified, these valiant mothers approached various corporate leaders and governmental authorities. There was a great deal of finger pointing. The bottom line was that nothing could be done because the cost of cleanup was astronomical. No corporate interest wanted to take it on, and the federal government, while identifying the site as a superfund site, had not allocated any funds for the cleanup. As a result, children's lives were being destroyed.

Such utter disregard for the human dignity and needs of families is heartbreaking. A pro-life stance would not allow such situations to continue unabated. It is painful to know that so many suffer the consequences of inaction and of policies that violate the dignity of individuals and families. As a person of faith, I wonder how corporations can let children suffer just to protect their bottom line, and how our government can turn a blind eye to this.

CONSEQUENCES OF SILENCE

Another unexpected result of my silence in the face of the extreme rhetoric—from both the far right and the far left—is that the opportunity for conversation about faith in progressive circles was lost for a couple of decades. My secular progressive friends love what we do at NETWORK but are befuddled as to how I approach this work through the lens of faith. They do not know how to integrate faith and their politics. They have come to believe the "sound bite" of the conservative talking points and Focus on the Family. In short, speaking of religion makes some secular progressives nervous. At the opposite end of the spectrum, at the same time, our political engagement with issues relating to the economy makes religious conservatives nervous. The truth is that we do not belong in either camp.

Indeed, we have become a small community that is in long-term tension with the dominant culture. We are a puzzle to the right and to the left. I pray that we will be able nurture the prophetic imagination that is not afraid of deeper truth and exterior conflict. We have a strong bond of community among ourselves that is both faithful and progressive. Ironically, it is a community to which many of my secular friends want to belong.

FAITH IN A SECULAR WORLD

When NETWORK relocated a few months ago, we had a ceremony to bless the new place. We invited many of our colleagues. Several people from the conservative religious channel EWTN as well as friends from our most secular progressive coalitions came. One young woman asked me who was going to bless the office. I may have scandalized her when I responded that we did not have a priest, but rather we were going to do the blessing together as a community.

We also made some of our colleagues nervous when we asked them to participate.

During a time of shared reflection in our new conference room we blessed the room and each other. Finally, as each person left the celebration, I invited them to take a moment to put some of our blessed water on our door, and, in their own way, to say a prayer and/or hold a thought that in our coming into and going out of this office we would be blessed in our work of fulfilling our mission.

One of my dearest memories of that blessing ritual occurred toward the end of the gathering. I noticed one of our super-secular colleagues leaving. He put his hand in the bowl of water and then placed it gently on the door. It was an act of tenderness, care, and a touch of the Divine.

When given a chance to connect with community, we hunger to belong. Our dignity is found in this web of relationships.

QUESTIONS FOR REFLECTION

Where am I in the conundrum of the issue of abortion?

What experiences have shaped my thinking? With whom do I talk about it?

For what public policies do I advocate in support of the dignity of life?

Do I see environmental laws as part of the protection of the dignity of life? Why or why not?

How can I/we bridge the perceived secular/religious divide?

11

Contemplative Action for Change

During 2016, I was involved in voter education efforts across the country. In Indianapolis, I met with a GED class of twenty-five adults. Each student was working toward obtaining his or her high school equivalency certificate. I asked the class about their concerns. They quickly identified two issues that particularly worried them: the level of wages and the cost of housing. In the process of the gentrification of their city, these amazing people were being pushed out of their neighborhoods.

After hearing their stories, I showed two ninety-second videos that we had prepared comparing the policy proposals of Secretary Clinton and then-candidate Donald Trump. The videos ended with me saying to the camera: "So you decide. Who is best for our nation? Who will you vote for on November 6?"

Immediately after the second video, Thomasina, a mother of two, blurted out, "Now I can vote! I wasn't going to vote because I was afraid I would hurt our country!" What did she mean? When I pursued this further with her, it became clear that all she knew about politics was based on the negative ads that she had seen on television. She did not know how to choose between the candidates, so she made the moral choice not to vote in order to avoid making a bad choice. Our short videos gave her actual information on which she could base an informed decision. I was stunned!

I had never considered the plight of people who are not intimately connected to politics! How can they vote when they really do not have any information beyond what they see on the television? I had formed a pre-conceived view about people who did not vote. I thought that they were "lazy" and just wanted to "coast" without paying the price of engaging with our democracy. By being open and willing to share with the students in the GED class, Thomasina taught me an entirely different truth.

Thomasina taught me that people do their best with what they have. In the course of our conversation after class, Thomasina told me that, as a child, she had never had new clothes for the first day of school. She was often teased on account of this. Because she did not want the same experience for her children, that year she sold her "clunker car" for $300 and used the money to buy her two children new clothes for school. She wanted them to start the school year without the stigma of "hand-me-downs." Thomasina was clearly a thoughtful mother engaged in making good choices for her children as well as for her nation. For me, it raised the question: How much are we doing to help Thomasina and those like her participate in our democracy?

It is clearly evident that we have work to do!

CHANGING THE WORLD

In his exhortation, *The Joy of the Gospel*, Pope Francis tells us: "An authentic faith—which is never comfortable or completely personal—always involves a deep desire to change the world, to transmit values, to leave this earth somehow better than we found it" (no. 184).

In the face of the political turmoil of the Trump era, my longing to leave the world better than I found it and the challenge of achieving this have been heightened.

Most important, in these chaotic times, a contemplative practice invites us to listen prayerfully. The practice of prayerful listening spills over into our daily life. It was this gift of listening that got me into a conversation with Thomasina, but it can happen for any of us at any time. The important part is to engage fully and remember to stay open.

Contemplative practice can help us listen to the experience of others without judgment...or, at the very least, to recognize our judgment and choose to open ourselves to another perspective. This is what happened with Thomasina. I was eager to pursue the conversation and understand her experience.

We need to recover the art of conversation, an art that rests on the contemplative practice of "holy curiosity." Holy curiosity is a much-needed virtue for the twenty-first century. This virtue involves being authentically interested in what another person thinks. A willingness to exercise curiosity through listening and asking follow-up questions has led me to the spiritual practice of "Grocery Store Missionary Work."

There are not many places where I stand in line, but one place where I do is at the grocery store. If there is a conversation in line, it is usually about the weather or a sports team. I like to begin a conversation by asking the person in front of or behind me a question about current events in order to learn that person's perspective. I will ask if she or he has opinion about raising wages, expanding health care, or voter suppression. I will ask about anything that is on my mind and in my heart and then listen to the response. I have discovered that while the general public has opinions on such topics, we are rarely in a position to hear from people we do not know. Practicing holy curiosity is one small step toward reweaving the fabric of our society. Democracy depends on an exchange of ideas.

SMALL SYSTEMIC CHANGE

When I was a young sister, there was in my community a hunger for "systemic change." We wanted to change the systems so that we could change the consequences for people living at the economic margins of our society. I had *big* ideas. Over the years, however, I have realized that creating massive change, such as passing the Affordable Care Act and being able to provide health care to twenty-three million more people in our country, happens rarely. Most legislative change is incremental. This has not changed my hunger for a big shift in wages or health care or housing, but it has made me more realistic.

The fact is that "structural change" does not have to be big. On our 2015 bus rip, we found ourselves in Little Rock, Arkansas, at an evening town hall. People were seated at round tables of eight to ten people and ready to engage in the discussion topics of the evening. The first step was to introduce yourself to your tablemates and say where you were from. One table group discovered they were all from the same neighborhood but did not know each other!

They engaged in an analysis of how they could all live within a few blocks of each other but not know each other or even recognize each other's faces. Upon reflection, they discovered a few things about their lifestyles. They learned that each of their homes has a garage that is attached to the house. Each of those garages has an automatic garage door opener. Each house has air conditioning. Many houses have their own backyard swimming pool. In short, each house is a self-contained unit that is not condusive to interaction with neighbors. As a result, they were cocooned in their own worlds.

A systemic change that they decided upon that night was to sit on their front porch (or front lawn, since some didn't have a porch) a couple of evenings a week and just wave at people who drove past. They thought that in this way they would at least have some awareness of who lived in their neighborhood.

It was with the participants at this table in Little Rock that I learned that systemic change in a community can start with small things. A simple awareness of who is in the community can be a first step toward real change. In fact, as long as I do not know who lives in the neighborhood, I am isolated and powerless.

Doing What You Can

A major consequence of the contemplative life is to be drawn into action by doing what you can, by doing the piece that has been given to you. In St. Louis, I met a group of African American women who call themselves "Mothers to Mothers." They had come together in 2014 after the police shooting of Michael Brown, an unarmed black youth. The killing horrified them. The atrocity was exacerbated by the fact that the police left Michael Brown's body uncovered in the street for hours. It represented a shocking disrespect for this young man.

The women knew that this could happen to any of their children. As mothers, they felt called to *do* something to change the racially charged reality in their city and state.

After considering their gifts, they decided that one thing they could do as a group of black mothers would be to talk with groups of white mothers about what black mothers had to worry about that white mothers did not. I will never forget the story we heard of one mother's conversation with her sons.

She told us about having "the talk" regularly with her sons, one of whom was in high school and the other in middle school. She quizzed them about what they would do *when* they were stopped by the police. (The issue was not *if* they were stopped, but *when*!) She had taught them that they needed to keep their hands out of their pockets and their arms away from their bodies. They needed to do what the police officer asked—and "not get any teenage attitude." Hearing of this training and her fear was heartbreaking. But then she reported that a week or so earlier her younger son had asked her, "Mommy, how long is this going to go on?" She said that she told him the truth. She added that, unless things changed dramatically in our country, this was going to go on for the rest of their lives.

These black women who wanted to *do* something were going to the white community and sharing with other mothers their reality. Their effort was to create a human connection between what happened to Michael Brown and the rest of their city. This was what they could do to make some change, and they did it! This is how change happens.

WORKERS IN THE VINEYARD

Meditation has consequences. Prayer leads us to community. Community leads us to action. Because we are listening to the needs of our world and not just our own needs, the action we take will often be "outside the box" of what we expect. What matters is that we act on what we hear. Sometimes we may feel timid and be tempted to procrastinate. We pray to open ourselves to the mystery of the Divine in our midst and then, at times, are reluctant to act. A fascinating fact is that, when we do act, our action can have effects far beyond what we could have imagined.

Recently, I was in Rome for an international meeting, and one of the sisters from the Philippines told me that Nuns on the Bus was known internationally! A sister from India chimed in to say that was absolutely true. Sisters from Senegal, Sweden, and Australia agreed. I was humbled and surprised. The Spirit shook us up here at NETWORK. Surprising things have happened. It has all been gift, even if there are days when I find myself weary and uncertain of how to respond.

We do not have to develop a "grand scheme" or have everything planned in detail. We need to do our part and be willing to be surprised. Surprise is a sign of the Spirit's presence with us. The creative Divine is still at work, and we are just collaborators in a much bigger project. We have to relinquish the desire to control and, in turn, open ourselves to the deeper story.

Our call to do our part is at the heart of the gospel message. We need to pitch in, listen to others, and stay open to the Spirit. We are the ones who have been sent out. The gospel of love will not be experienced unless we live the deeply contemplative truth that our prayer leads to community, which leads to action to heal this fractured world.

So, let your heart be broken open by the anguish of our time. Come together in community and listen for the "still, small voice" that can give you direction. Trust those with whom you travel to share your commitment. Finally, act on what you hear. You do not have to do it all; you only have to do your part. Break out of the individualism of our time that says: "We are the messiahs." We are not. We are only workers in the vineyard.

Maybe our world is like a giant jigsaw puzzle and each of us is a piece of this complex puzzle. Be your piece. Do your part. Trust that others, with your support, will do their part. Then we will be faithful, and our world, ever so slightly, but meaningfully, will be changed.

QUESTIONS FOR REFLECTION

How does my contemplative practice lead me to act for change?

In my contemplation, what actions am I led to take in order to engage the needs of my community?

Have I prayed using the newspaper or online blogs?

What effect does holding a situation in my heart with compassion have on me?

Conclusion

My experience of the contemplative life frequently feels like searching aimlessly in the dark. When I am seeking answers or direction, I often attempt to squeeze out some insight. It is like being caught near the bank of a river where there is a small whirlpool generated by a deeper hole or a large boulder. I now recognize that this happens when I try to be in control. I want to set the agenda. I want to be the one to see clearly. I want to be in charge.

The moment of hunger for control is when I most need to surrender—to let go and trust that the Spirit is alive and well...and making mischief. I just cannot see it yet. After loosening my grasping desire for control, I sense that I am back in the middle of the river, floating in the current of the unseen divine presence. This is living in trust that the gifts we need are given before we know we need them. Experiencing this life in the river moves me beyond individualism and into a sense of the collective. It once again reinforces the truth that Sr. Ilia Delio has noted: "The Church does not exist for itself, it exists for the world." So too, our contemplative practice is not for ourselves, but for the sake of our famished world.

Contemplative practice is needed now in our chaotic times and in the midst of a world that has become polarized. Our time demands a new measure of fidelity. We are not called to see the full road ahead; we are called only to keep moving. On the first day of recollection that I made when I joined the Sisters of Social Service, the retreat director said: "Faith is like walking through the mist with your eyes wide open!"

This mist may seem impenetrable at times and it may make it difficult for us to evaluate our actions and engagement. There are days when we may experience utter frustration. But we cannot stop. For me, the fact that my ministry over these last sixteen years has been at NETWORK has been a great gift. I have been able to work directly with Congress and three different presidential administrations. Because of my political engagement, I have a strong sense of purpose and community. It is in this engagement that I encounter hope.

Today's political crisis reflects the reality that, as a people, we are not in the center of the river with a strong sense of each other or of mission. Contemplative practice for the sake of the whole can help us find our way forward even through the dim light of today's world. Communal fidelity is the wellspring of hope, which is a shared virtue and the anchor of holiness in the twenty-first century.

I never think about being holy. I think only about being faithful. However, Pope Francis's exhortation on holiness has stirred in me an awareness that there are some characteristics we need to nourish if we are to be faithful. Our hope resides in our faithfulness. I want to examine several characteristics mentioned in the exhortation, characteristics that can serve as touchstones for our lives in discerning whether we are on the right track. They are communal virtues and a good way to gauge if we are living in response to the call of our time.

Perseverance and Meekness

If our hearts are broken open to suffering, we cannot cease our engagement for justice. This does not necessarily mean that we continue to be engaged in the same ways as when we were younger, but it does mean that we continue to be engaged.

One of my good friends in community, who is now in her mid-nineties, continues to email important articles to our whole community. Her prayer is a regular witness to us. Her emails help the rest of us stay engaged. She perseveres in the face of adversity. A newer member of our community perseveres in her ministry as an attorney for asylum seekers even in the face of the Trump administration's policy of doing everything possible to prevent these traumatized people from entering our country.

Perseverance is also required in the work we do to promote policies that are just. The struggle for health care and economic justice for everyone requires constant focus. In the political realm, I know that inching forward and slipping back are part of the process, but it is perseverance that will bring change. It took one hundred years of trying to pass legislation in Congress to extend health care to more of our people. The Affordable Care Act is not perfect, but it is an important step forward. We are called to persevere in protecting and extending health care to all in need.

Our small organization, NETWORK, practiced perseverance when confronted with the criticism from the Vatican in 2012. Rather than getting sidetracked by the criticism and engaging in an ecclesial conflict, we stayed focused on our mission of embodying the social teaching of the church. While this was a challenge, our faithful perseverance yielded much fruit and resulted in our being catapulted to a much higher level of impact and influence. This was all thanks to the Vatican and our effort to be faithful to mission.

In his apostolic exhortation, "Rejoice and be Glad," Pope Francis notes that, along with perseverance, meekness is required. In fact, "meekness is yet another expression of the interior poverty of those who put their trust in God alone" (no. 74). For Francis, meekness is the ability to learn from others. In the practice of perseverance, we must be willing to learn from others, which means that we must be willing to listen to them.

In 2014, I met Laurie, a woman in her early thirties who was doing community organizing in Colorado Springs. As part of our Nuns on the Bus stop there, she and I spent several hours together, knocking on doors to turn out the vote. As we were walking along, she told me her story. A few years earlier, she had come out to her family as a lesbian. Her father, a Southern Baptist minister, was horrified. Her family sent her away for "de-programing" at Focus on the Family. She described her six months in the program as excruciating torture. Finally, she ran away from the program. She found a good counselor, got her bearings, and began to discern for herself what mattered. She discovered her value as an individual. I was struck by how she persevered to find her true self.

But Laurie taught me an even more powerful lesson of meekness. Rather than rail against the treatment she had received from her father, she recognized that the work she was doing as a community organizer was similar to his work as a Baptist pastor: she visited people; she listened to their stories; and she comforted and planned with them for a better future.

I was amazed that Laurie was able to see in herself the gifts of someone who had rejected her so painfully. Her wonderful meekness in being willing to learn from her father was a witness to me about gospel holiness. Yes, we must persevere in our efforts to create justice, but we are also called to learn from each other, even from the people who have hurt us. Such meekness is the seedbed of hope.

JOY AND A SENSE OF HUMOR

Those of us who strive for justice in today's world are often grim and morose. We can recount the latest atrocities in the world. We can expound on the commentaries aired on television. We lament the violence and division around us. We are often angry and rail against the atrocities of our time. Sometimes we even rail at allies for not being as outraged as we are. I have heard more than once the carp: "Can't you take this seriously?" We can be depressed. And with our grim faces, full of lamentation, we then ask our friends to come and join us in this work. Our demeanor is not always a positive advertisement for the work of justice. Grimness is not an expression of twenty-first century holiness.

In his exhortation, *The Joy of the Gospel*, Pope Francis notes: "Whenever our interior life becomes caught up in its own interests and concerns, there is no longer room for others, no place for the poor. God's voice is no longer heard, the quiet joy of his love is no longer felt, and the desire to do good fades" (no. 2).

Life in the Spirit draws us into joy in relationship. As Nuns on the Bus we experience this joy of engagement repeatedly on our trips. Woven together in community and a common purpose, we bring community with us and have it reflected back at us at every bus stop. At every destination we find welcoming joy.

On the bus, our joy is rooted in a daily practice of contemplative prayer. We gather for half an hour in the morning before heading out on the road. In 2012, the first year of the bus trips, we gathered for prayer the first three mornings, but on the fourth day we had a very early start. The intensity of the trip had tired us out. We decided that, rather than pray together before getting on the bus, we would pray after we got on the bus. It was a great plan.

However, once we were on the bus, we immediately got caught up in the business of the day—dealing with the press, phone calls, prepping for the next stop, and so on. We did not pray.

By mid-afternoon we were snapping at each other. We did not have the interior space to deal with the close confines of the bus and the various pressures we were experiencing. It was then that I made the resolution that we would never miss our morning prayer again...and we have not. This has been a life-saving decision.

Shared prayer with our "bus" community weaves us together and gives us the space to know that it is the Spirit that is at the heart of the work. In prayer, we come to a place where we do not take ourselves too seriously and are willing to learn from each other and from those we meet. The commitment to grounding our work each morning in contemplative practice has provided us with a daily experience of the sacred, a solid foundation for responding with meekness to those we encounter. It has enabled us to laugh often and spread a gospel of joy in a very troubled world. On the bus, we live and breathe the deep hope of community.

PASSION AND BOLDNESS

Pope Francis refers to a third communal virtue: passion and boldness. Our age is not a time for timidity. Contemplative practice enables us to have "next steps" sensed, almost revealed. This may seem absurd to someone unfamiliar with contemplative practice, but in prayer, it seems both reasonable and obvious.

When I practiced law, many of my colleagues would tell me that I made "outrageous" arguments in applying the law to the facts. They found it annoying that these arguments would often get favorable rulings from the judge. It was contemplative practice that gave me the capacity to think "outside the box" in the practice of law.

I experienced something similar when I spoke at the Democratic National Convention. While the process of getting to speak there had been fraught with conflict, once consensus had been achieved with regard to my addressing the convention, I was able to walk onstage trusting that the Spirit was at the heart of the moment. For me, at the time, the Spirit was embodied in the man I met backstage just before I went out to speak. He chatted with me and asked if I needed water. He took me into the wings to view the stage and the crowd. He told me to "own the moment" and "wave as you go out." He grounded me in the moment and the mission of that time. He was evidence that the Spirit was not leaving me orphaned. His whispered words inspired confidence and allowed me to relax in the Spirit and speak from the heart.

Another example of contemplative practice in action is this book. Through it, I am sharing my insights of the Spirit alive in the community. If we but attend to this deep truth, we will be given the insights necessary to act in ways that can change the trajectory of our society. This is not a time for timidity. The urgency of now requires us to recognize the needs of our world and respond as best we can. It is not a time for procrastination. We need to listen deeply in community and speak up with what we hear. Holiness is contagious when lived with passion and boldness.

COMMUNITY

The fourth characteristic mentioned by Pope Francis is living the gospel in community. As noted earlier, it is community that is the antidote to the hyper-individualism of our time. The contemplative questions become: Whom can I lean on, and who leans on me? Who has my back, and whom do I look out for? Who is there for me, and whom do I care for? In short, whom do I hold in my heart?

For me, the answers are my religious community, other Catholic sisters, my family, and more. Recently I had a surprising experience of community. I have been a member of a sewing circle in Oakland since 1983. The group consists of five women who at one point actually sewed. We originally met because we had some connection with the legal field. We were women hungering for support in a male-dominated profession. The relationships that resulted have been profound.

In the beginning, I did tailoring and made all my suits. One of our members makes dolls to tell the story of her African American heritage. Another member does amazing art pieces including portraits. Her work has been "collected" by art museums. A fourth member made jackets in a kimono style. Our fifth member protests that she does not actually sew. We say that she mends, and that qualifies. For years, we met on alternate Wednesdays and shared life and grew close. When I left Oakland, the group did not meet as often, but we have stayed close. We still meet whenever I am in the Oakland area and we can arrange it and, and we have continued to be in touch through social media.

Recently, one of our beloved members had a severe medical crisis. It is a miracle that she is even alive. But the reality galvanized us into action for her care. I, because of time zones, was the first to receive the message about the crisis. I reached out to the others and had a conversation with each one. The response from each one of them was: "I'm going to the hospital," even though our member in crisis was going to be in surgery. The need to gather was palpable. It was excruciating for me to be a continent and three time zones away, but it led us to coalesce through shared text messages and conference calls. It also got me to make a quick trip to Oakland to physically connect with my people as soon as possible. I realized that we are one organism, all turned toward the hurt of one part. We were acting for the healing of one which quickly became the healing of all of us. We were like a sunflower turning toward the sun. We are a community that cannot look away; we are there for each other.

The experience of being a single organism with my friends allowed me to experience the visceral hunger to be physically connected. Now, through email and text messages, we are working out how we can be a support to each other in challenging times. It is work to support our member in her healing. We are having to learn new skills but, as a loving and supportive organism, we are adapting and letting the love of our connection carry us forward into mystery. Ironically, none of my fellow sewing circle members share my faith or my perspective on faith, but I do know that we share the experience of being one body in caring for and loving each other.

Community is the anchor that can help us through challenging times. It is the foundation of our best selves. It is the life-giving source of nourishment for the long haul. This is the fruit of having our hearts broken open and recognizing hope in our midst. It is the energy of being one organism in a challenging time.

Constant Prayer

The final characteristic that Pope Francis mentions is the challenge to live in constant prayer. In reality, this means knowing that, at every moment, we need help. Often my prayer is just that: HELP!

The listening sessions we held in 2019 with rural communities allowed us to hear first-hand the stories of rural residents in our nation and then to share them with "city folks" to try to create some healing and understanding. Our managing director, Paul Marchione, had suggested that we use a roundtable format in rural communities because of our success in having done "business roundtables" a few years earlier. It was total intuition... or an answer to prayer. We did not know what we were going to do with the information or how it might affect us. We went with holy curiosity to receive the stories. I trusted that we would be led.

As a result of my giving a talk in DC and mentioning the rural roundtables, the next step was revealed. Someone who was present at that talk knew and put us in touch with former Senator Heitkamp, who is now working on rural issues since she no longer represents North Dakota in the US Senate. Senator Heitkamp is eager to support our work and make sure that our information gets published and becomes part of the 2020 election cycle conversation. Now we are working with her team to share what we have learned.

For me, this came about because we have been open to the Spirit and breathed the consistent mantra: Help! Every breath is a breath of trust and surrender. We are woven together in community, and someone is able to sustain that prayer every day. As long as one of us is engaged in prayer, the whole community will struggle toward the transformation at the heart of the Gospel: Love one another.

Final Word

Our world of violence and discord is in dire need of a contemplative presence. We are called to take in the mystery of others and weave community into the fabric of our time. We are called to be one organism, one body in this very challenging moment of the twenty-first century. We are called to the joy at the heart of it all because we are hummed into existence by the Divine at every moment. This is the source of our hope. We are not left orphans. No! We are woven into a family where we can bring our broken hearts, our curiosity, our sense of history, and our willingness to engage. Together, we constitute the prophetic imagination for which we hunger. Let us open ourselves to the truth all around us. The Divine comes to us in the locked rooms of individualistic fear and says, "Peace!"

The Divine appears as fire, impelling us to go out into the world to bring good news to the poor. It is those whom we encounter and who break open our hearts who keep us faithful. Together we know our existence as one vibrant organism created at every moment by the Divine. This is the source of a hope beyond our wildest understanding.

Our contemplative practice helps us see the deeper truth: our hunger for hope keeps us on the road toward justice; our hunger for hope leads us to know the promise of Isaiah that the blind will see, the lame will walk, and the poor will have the gospel preached to them. In short, our hunger for hope will be satisfied.

Resources for the Journey

BOOKS

Brueggemann, Walter. *The Prophetic Imagination*, 2nd ed. Minneapolis, MN: Fortress, 2001.

Campbell, Simone. *A Nun on the Bus: How All of Us Can Create Hope, Change, and Community*. New York: Harper One, 2014.

Delio, Ilia. *Making All Things New: Catholicity, Cosmology, Consciousness*. Maryknoll, NY: Orbis Books, 2016.

Johnson, Elizabeth. *Quest for the Living God*. New York: Bloomsbury Academic, 2007.

May, Gerald. *Will and Spirit: A Contemplative Psychology*. New York, Harper Collins, 1987.

Diangelo, Robin. *White Fragility: Why It Is So Hard for White People to Talk about Racism*. Boston: Beacon, 2018.

Wilkinson, Richard, and Kate Pickett. *The Spirit Level*, New York: Bloomsbury, 2010.

Pope Francis: *Laudato Si'*, *Evangelii Gaudium*, *Gaudete et Exsultate*.

ON LINE RESOURCES

Rohr, Richard. Center for Action and Contemplation, www.cac.org.

Sylvester, Nancy. Institute for Communal Contemplation and Dialogue, www.iccdinstitute.org.

Contemplative Outreach (resources for a contemplative/centering prayer practice). www.contemplativeoutreach.org.

Zen Mountain Monastery and Zen Center of New York City. "How to Meditate." www.zmm.org.